MW00605939

CHANGE YOUR *Questions* CHANGE YOUR LIFE

Other Titles by Wendy Watson Nelson

Books

Purity and Passion: Spiritual Truths about Intimacy That Will Strengthen Your Marriage

Rock-Solid Relationships: Strengthening Personal Relationships with Wisdom from the Scriptures

Talks on CD

Let Your Spirit Take the Lead

The Savior Heals without a Scar (with Sheri Dew)

Things Are Not Always As They Appear

Webinar

Change Your Questions, Change Your Life

TimeOutLifeSeminars.com/Wendy

CHANGE YOUR *Questions* CHANGE YOUR LIFE

WENDY WATSON NELSON

SALT LAKE CITY, UTAH

Visit us at DeseretBook.com

Library of Congress Cataloging-in-Publication Data

Nelson, Wendy Watson, 1950–
Change your questions, change your life / Wendy Watson Nelson.
p. cm.
Includes bibliographical references.
ISBN 978-1-59038-598-2 (hardbound : alk. paper)
1. Questioning. 2. Introspection—Religious aspects—Church of Jesus Christ of Latter-day Saints. 3. Self-actualization (Psychology)—Religious aspects—Church of Jesus Christ of Latter-day Saints. 4. Christian life—Mormon authors. I. Title.
BX8656.N44 2009
248.4'893—dc22 2009034331

Printed in China
R. R. Donnelley, Shenzhen, China
10 9 8 7 6 5 4 3 2 1

For Elder Russell M. Nelson

who, with one question, changed my life–

turning it upside down, or as he likes to say–

turning it right side up!

CONTENTS

CHAPTER 1 THE POWER OF QUESTIONS

SEEING IT AS IT IS

Questions can be powerful!
Questions can help us see things we haven't seen before!

It was a photo I took of a leopard that most recently taught me this truth.

I was with my husband on a game park in South Africa. We had a guide and a tracker and we were traveling in an open Land Rover. (The operative word is *open*.)

This was my view as we traveled through the South African wilderness. Note the gun. This was no Disney safari!

We spotted elephants and zebras and giraffes. We were very close to the animals and the guide told us how to remain safe:

KEEP YOUR ARMS AND HANDS INSIDE THE VEHICLE. BE QUIET AND DON'T STAND UP TO VIEW THE ANIMALS. THEY ARE USED TO THE SHAPE OF THE VEHICLE AND WILL LEAVE US ALONE AS LONG AS THE SHAPE STAYS THE SAME.

There was no question about my willingness to be compliant.

We drove for hours on end, very early in the morning and in the evening. The cold of the desert was intense, and we layered every item of clothing we had brought—and then borrowed more. As we roamed the land our eyes became more able to spot camouflaged animals, and our ears heard the rustling of creatures more quickly. Upon sighting an animal or grouping, our tracker and guide would position our vehicle as close as possible to the animals.

Here is the evidence of their success: 

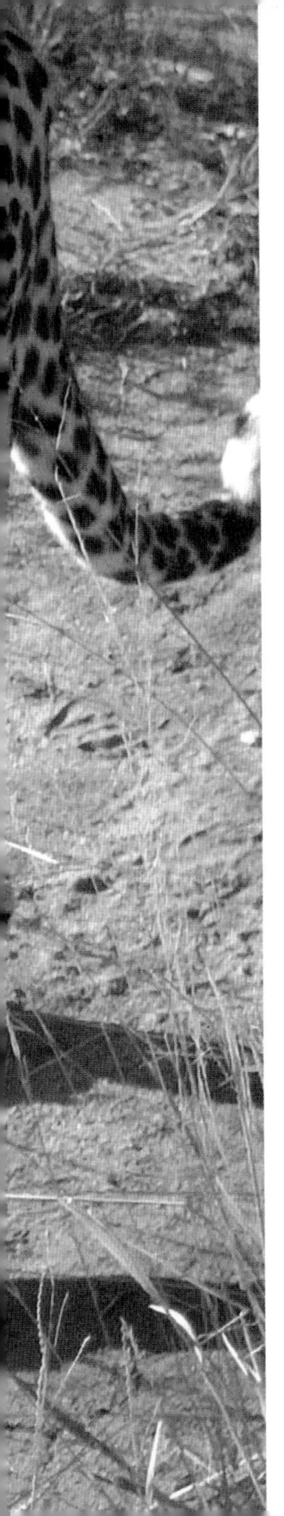

I gasped when I saw this photo. And I had taken it! I don't own a sophisticated camera with a huge telephoto lens. Mine is a small digital camera I can hold in my hand. It is great for family photos. So when I got home from the trip and was reviewing my photos in the safety of my living room, I saw something I had *not* seen before.

While taking the photo, I had known we were very close to the animal—so close that I could have literally patted that leopard's head. But looking at the photo made me realize *just* how close we had been, and it made me shudder, especially when I recalled what my husband said as the animal walked away: "I didn't like the way that leopard was looking at you!"

Looking at the photo, I could see exactly how he had been looking at me. And I didn't like it, either. *Why hadn't I seen it at the time?*

The reality revealed through the photo allowed me to see something I hadn't seen in the actual live moment. Looking at the photograph now was like getting a whack on the side of my head, and I asked myself:

WHAT WAS I DOING IN SUCH A DANGEROUS SITUATION?

At the time it hadn't seemed that dangerous. But with some distance and some reflection—both of which the photo provided—the danger of the situation was undeniable.

Perhaps that's similar to other situations in our lives.

We live with them day after day—until something causes us to see ourselves and the situation in a new way, and we recognize the danger for what it is: Life-threatening. Spirituality-threatening. Relationship-threatening. And we know that a change is urgently needed.

I shared the experience with a group of women. One wrote the following in a note to me:

"The story you shared of your experience with the leopard has given me something that I cannot adequately describe but that was, and is, essential to my future and every choice I make from here on out. Truly no exaggeration."

What? A story about a photo of a leopard caught a woman's mind and heart in such a way that it will now influence her future and every choice she will make from here on out? Really? How could that be?

Her note continued:

"That you did not recognize how dangerous the situation was while *you were in it, but only* after *you saw the photograph of the leopard, is analogous to my life. Your leopard-picture story helped me today because I will no longer feel stupid or inept for living in a dangerous situation for the time I did. I no longer feel defective.*

"Intellectually, I've already recognized that I was in a survival mode and simply did not connect to any fear. But emotionally *I've been berating myself for not* recognizing *and taking* action *sooner. No longer will I berate myself. I did the best I could! And I left as* soon *as I* knew *what was* really *going on. When I saw the full* picture."

Asking great questions does just that.

Great questions allow us to see a fuller picture.

Great questions can motivate us to change because they invite us to reflect. They help us to see some part of ourselves or others or a situation we've never been able to see before!

A wise Chilean biologist defined the term "reflection" in exactly that way:

"The moment of reflection . . . is the moment when we become aware of that part of ourselves which we cannot see in any other way."[1]

The Savior invited the men who were ready to stone a woman to reflect—to see a part of themselves that they could not see in any other way. As the scribes and the Pharisees railed on about the punishment a woman "taken in sin" should receive, Jesus stooped down and traced with His finger on the ground. He invited them to take a close look at *themselves* by saying, "He that is without sin among you, let him first cast a stone at her" (John 8:7). The men judged themselves and slunk away in shame and disgrace.

The power of questions comes from their ability to invite us to reflect!

If you want a great experience with questions, and with being invited over and over again to reflect upon your life, read Alma 5. There are at least forty questions within that one chapter. I never seem to be able to get an accurate count because Alma's questions are so effective that I start thinking and reflecting . . . and I lose count.

Read Alma 5
and select your favorite questions.
Then answer them.

Alma invites us to look at our lives through the mirror of the Lord—the most important mirror of all. Alma invites us to reflect upon our standing before the Lord and increase our desire to change and to be better—all through the use of great questions!

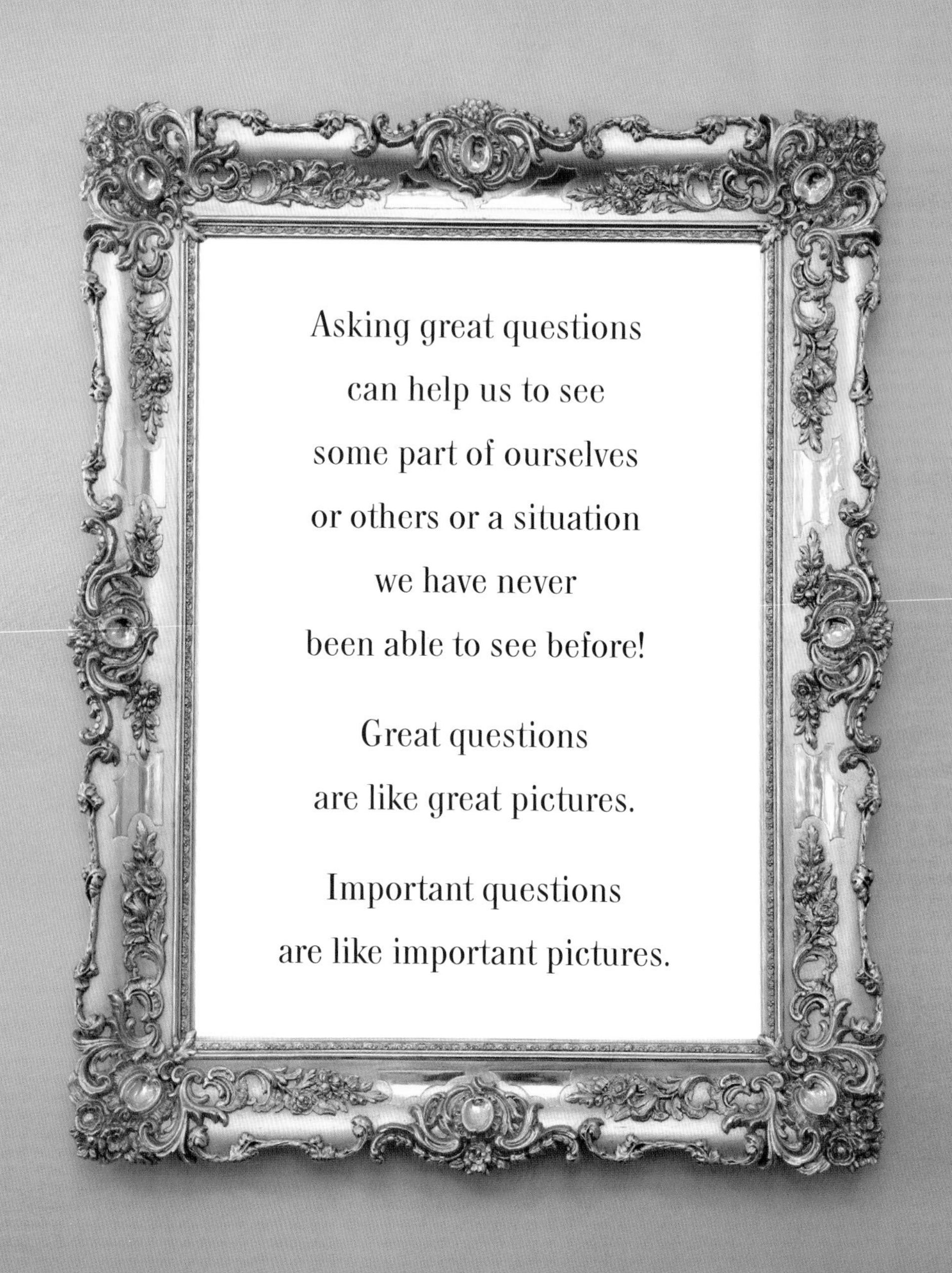
Asking great questions
can help us to see
some part of ourselves
or others or a situation
we have never
been able to see before!
Great questions
are like great pictures.
Important questions
are like important pictures.

Have you ever looked at a photo of yourself and suddenly seen something about yourself you had never seen before? Perhaps it was your slumped posture or your sagging belly or the scowl on your face—when all this time you thought you were standing straight, were very trim, and were smiling and looking as approachable as you felt?

The picture invited you to a shocking reflection.

Questions invite us to reflect.

I think of a father who was dutifully helping one of his children get ready for bed. He barked out order after order: "Brush your teeth. Wash your hands. Put on your pajamas." Suddenly his young daughter turned to him and asked a question: *"Do you own me, Daddy?"*

Oh, the power of a child's question to invite a father to reflect and to repent.

I think also of a grandmother who at Christmastime was hurrying and scurrying to get everything done. She was exhausted. It was very late at night and yet she still had one more gingerbread house to make. She was determined to get it done. In the midst of her focused frenzy, her little four-year-old granddaughter turned to her and asked, "Grandma, are you mad at me?"

"No, dear. I'm not mad. I'm just very tired."

Then the little girl asked a question that invited her grandmother to see herself in quite a stark way. The little girl asked, *"Well, Grandma, do you know that when you're tired, your voice raises?"*

I LOVE Questions!

I love their ability to help us focus.

To see things we've never seen before.

To understand things we've never understood before.

To think things we've never thought before.

To have the courage to do things we've never had the courage to do before.

What are your questions doing for you?

Are your questions enlivening you?

Encouraging you?

Enlarging your life?

Expanding your vision?

Enriching your relationships?

Are your questions depressing you? Discouraging and demoralizing you?
Are your questions inviting fear or joy into your life? Energy or frustration?

IF YOU WANT TO CHANGE YOUR LIFE, CHANGE YOUR QUESTIONS!

IF YOU WANT A GREAT LIFE,
ASK GREAT QUESTIONS!

Now, let's step back for a moment and talk about questions in general.

What has a more positive influence on you? A statement, such as: *You look great!*

Or the question: *Have you been working out?*

Which might be more encouraging? A statement: *You are so good!* Or a question: *Are you as good as you look?*

Questions can be soothing, such as a question we coo to a baby: *Why are you so adorable?*

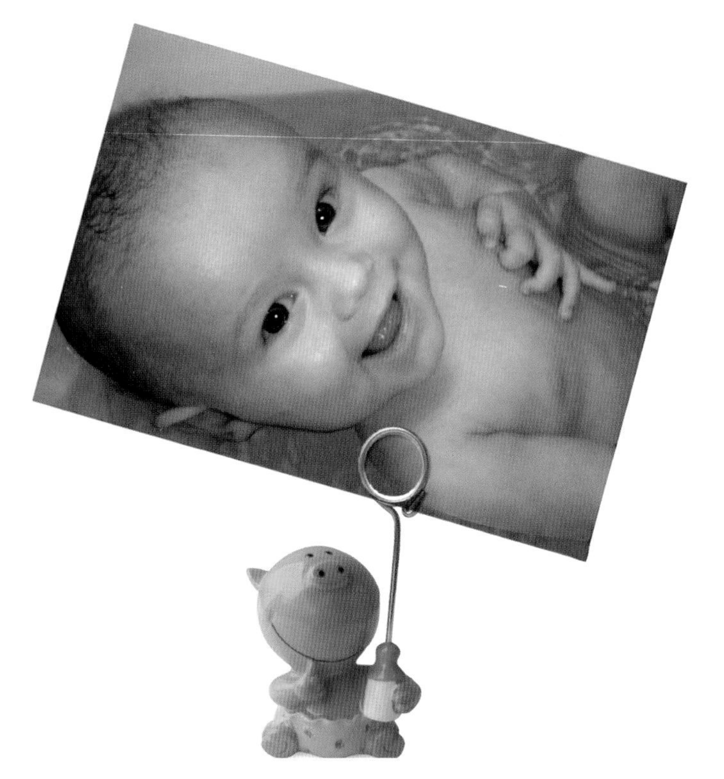

Questions can be fortifying, such as a question we may say to a dear friend: *Why am I so blessed to have you in my life?*

Questions can be endearing, such as a question we might whisper to a spouse: *Do you know how much I love you?*

The question lingers a little bit longer than the statement *I love you,* doesn't it?

Embedding a statement within a question can strengthen the statement.

Some questions can stop us dead in our tracks, such as the question a wife in a cartoon asks her husband. He is attempting to offer her an apology when she interrupts him and asks: *How do you dare apologize to me after what you did?*

Can you feel the mind-freezing effect of such a question?

Some questions can be guilt-inducing and immobilizing: *Why can't I ever trust you to do what you say you will do?*

Or comforting: *What can I do to help you today? What would lighten your load?*

Some questions are just for the moment: *Would you like fries with that?*

And the effect of others can linger for years—such as the agonizing questions parents may punish themselves with following the death of their child by suicide: *Why did he kill himself? Where did we go wrong? Why didn't we do something when we saw him changing?*

Some questions can cut through very difficult and highly charged situations, such as the question Brigham Young humbly asked Joseph Smith after being falsely accused by the Prophet in public. Instead of defending himself Brigham asked, "*What do you want me to do?*"[2]

Questions can indeed have a powerful effect!

Let me share a personal example. Some might call me a "creative cook." I am not fond of following recipes and some of my concoctions are more appealing than others. I'll admit that in my best efforts to make something delicious for dinner, sometimes I get a little carried away with the ingredients I put together. My husband consistently handles these precarious dining situations with loving kindness. As I bring to him my latest creation, he asks one question that always warms my heart and makes me laugh:

Now, honey, if we were at a restaurant and wanted to order this, what would we call it?

What a marvelous spirit-lifting and relationship-building question!

Unfortunately, some questions can CAUSE trouble!

Let's consider the troublemaking question that begins, "Why am I so . . . ?" and ends with any number of self-demoralizing, hating, flogging, defeating, disdaining, or sabotaging words or phrases. Most of us don't need much help writing a negative kind of question, do we?

Ask yourself, "Is there a troublemaking, havoc-wreaking question in my life that sneaks up on me from time to time that begins with *Why am I so . . . ?*"

Troublemaking questions are spiritually weakening.

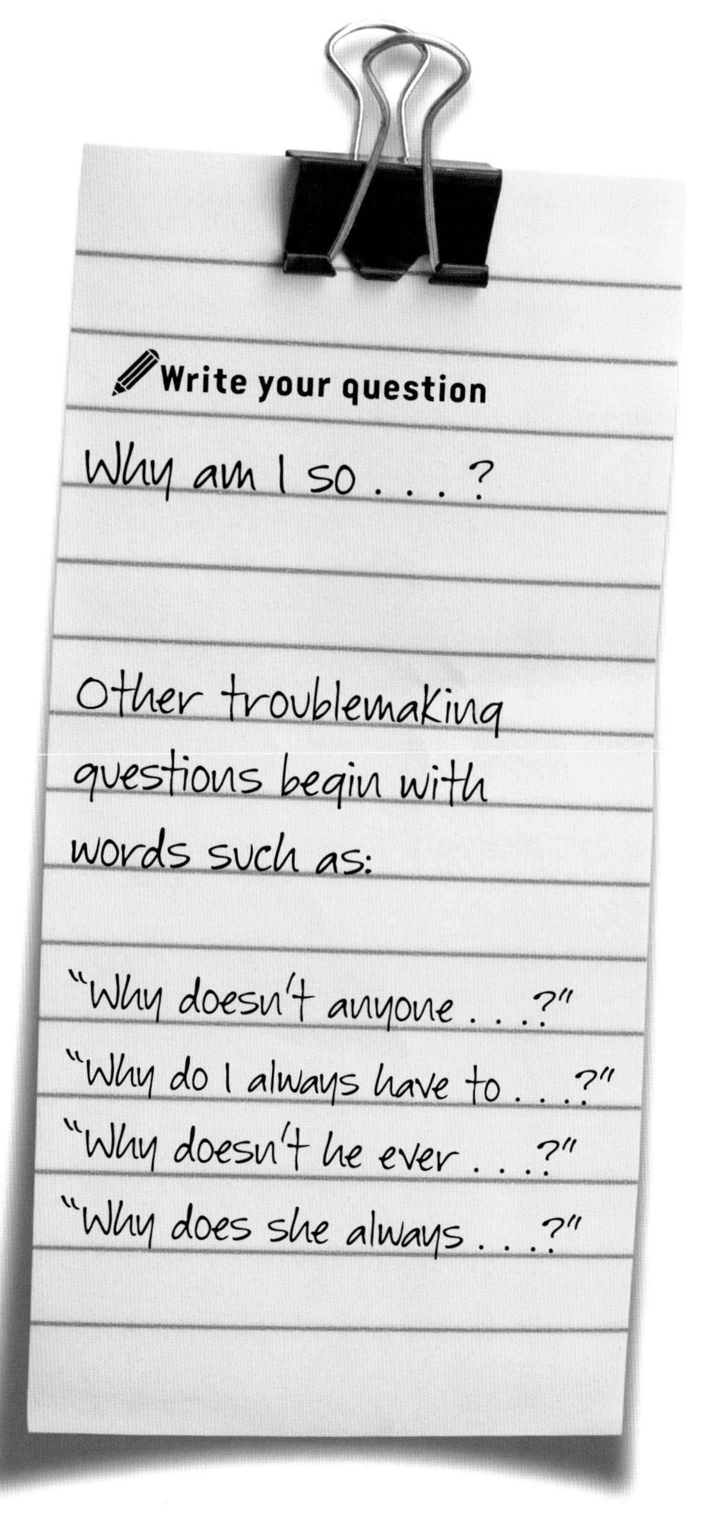

Think about

What troublemaking questions do you presently ask yourself, others, or the Lord that invite the 4 Ds into your life and relationships?

If you wanted to have a real "pity party" with the 4 Ds present, what questions would you ask yourself to guarantee that doubt, discouragement, depression, and despair would show up in your mind and in your heart?

Write about

What questions cause trouble for you?
Can you list some of them?
Write them down so you can see them.

Which question is the biggest bully in your life?

Which one pushes you around the most
and causes you the most trouble?

Which question has been holding
you back from moving ahead
with your life?

Think about

Now, think about the influence of those troublemaking questions on you, your life, and your relationships.

What do they invite you to think, to feel, and to do?

Well, now, are you ready for some change?

DO YOU WANT TO CHANGE YOUR LIFE?
THEN CHANGE YOUR QUESTIONS!

?
DO YOU WANT BETTER
RELATIONSHIPS?

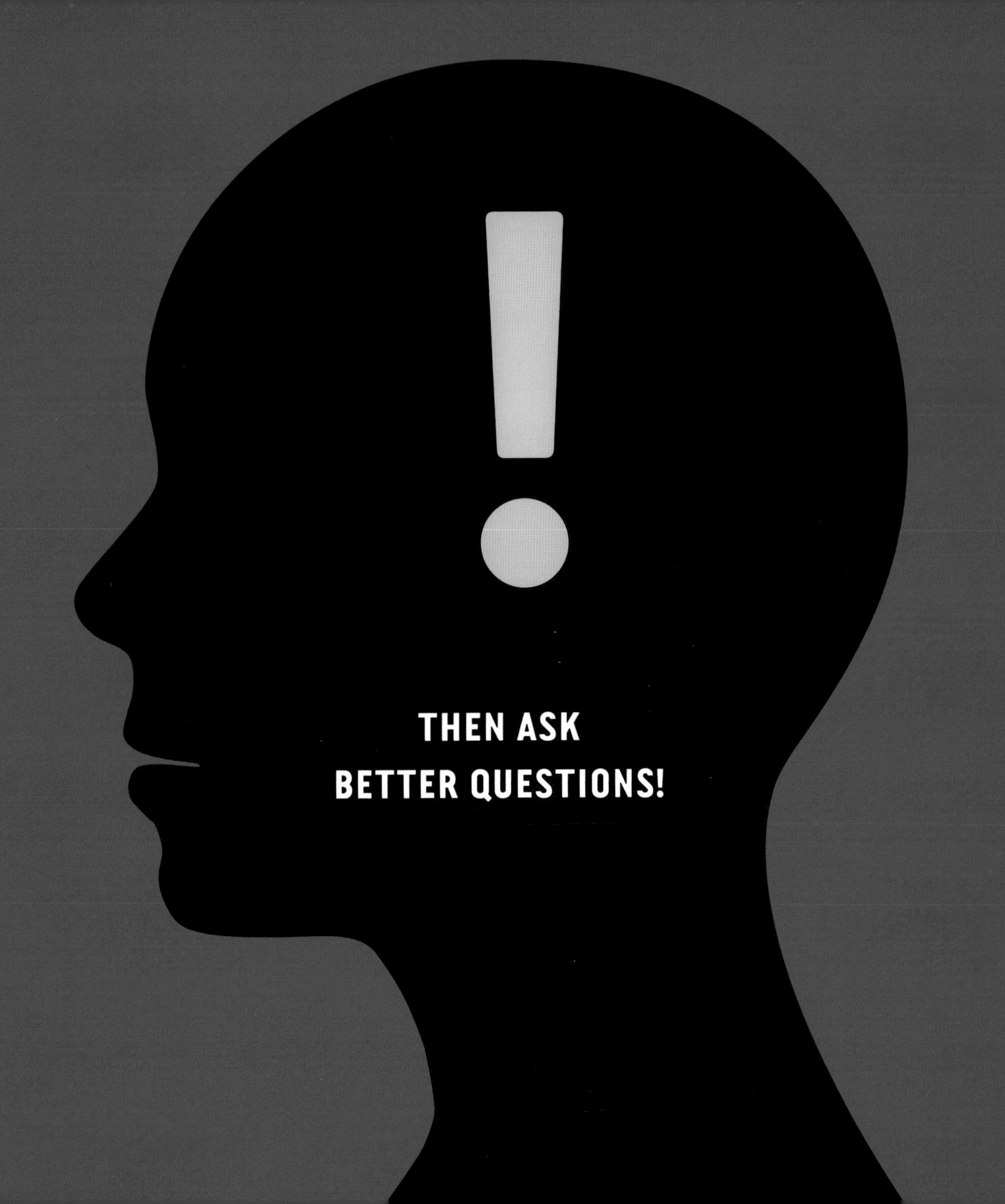
THEN ASK
BETTER QUESTIONS!

JUNE

Wednesday

Consider the questions that President Henry B. Eyring counseled us to ask ourselves on a daily basis:

- "Have I seen the hand of God reaching out to touch [me] or [my] children or [my] family today?"
- "Did God send a message that was just for me?"
- What can I do "to preserve that memory for the day that I, and those I love, will need to remember how much God loves us and how much we need Him"?[3]

Imagine the effect it would have in your life if you were to consistently ask yourself these three great questions.

- What would you begin to notice?
- What would you begin to remember?

The truth is that the Lord wants you to have a great life and the adversary doesn't!

Simply put, the adversary wants you to be as miserable as he is.

The apostle Peter said it so well:

"Be sober, be vigilant; because your adversary the devil, as a roaring lion, walketh about, seeking whom he may devour" (1 Peter 5:8).

The adversary wants to devour your life! He wants to destroy you and everything you came to mortality to do. And he wants to devour your relationships!

Now, I don't know about the roaring lions of which Peter speaks, but I do know about the ravaging leopard that prowls about seeking whom he may devour. In fact, a chilling follow-up to the story of our safari is that the day after we had that very up close and a little too personal meeting with the leopard, an employee was attacked and killed by a leopard in the camp right next to ours!

So I would echo and slightly adapt Peter's words to say:

"Be sober, be vigilant, because your adversary the devil, as a ravaging leopard, walketh about, seeking whom he may devour!"

It's a jungle out there—literally and figuratively. Make no mistake about it.

As a way to ensure our survival, the apostle Paul urged us to *"Put on the whole armour of God, that ye may be able to stand against the wiles of the devil"* (Ephesians 6:11).

Asking ourselves great questions, useful questions, inspired questions, and truth-filled questions can help us put on our essential protecting armor.

The following words by President Henry B. Eyring speak of the reality and urgency for protection:

"As the forces around us increase in intensity, whatever spiritual strength was once sufficient, will not be enough."[4]

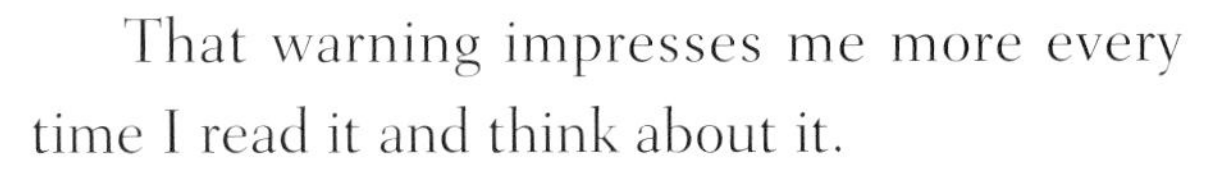

That warning impresses me more every time I read it and think about it.

Whatever spiritual strength was once sufficient to build a great life in the '50s, '60s, '70s, '80s, and '90s will not be enough now in the twenty-first century.

Whatever spiritual strength was once sufficient to build a great marriage won't be enough today.

Whatever spiritual strength was once sufficient to protect our families won't be now—not now that the forces attacking our lives, our marriages, and our families are exponentially increasing.

We need to counter the insidious and relentless attack on our lives, our marriages, and our families by dramatically increasing our spiritual strength daily.

The questions we ask ourselves, others, and the Lord can help us do just that!

Think about

. . . some of the questions in your life.

1. In the last 24 hours, what is one question you asked yourself?
2. Is there a question you long for someone to ask you?
3. Think of someone with whom you want to build a stronger relationship. What questions do you typically ask them during the first few minutes you are together?
4. What is the last question you asked the Lord?

Take a few minutes and answer those questions about the questions in your life.

Now think about . . .

What effect do your questions have on your spirit and on the spirits of those you love?
Do your questions build and lift?
Are they likely to strengthen others spiritually?

Some questions can bring about change when everything else has failed.

Let me give you an example:

I once spoke about the power of questions with a group in Hawaii, and the next day a woman—let's call her Sally—came to me and told me her story. She had come to my class quite preoccupied because of a troublesome situation with her dearest friend—let's call her Carol—who lived on the mainland. The conflict arose when Carol called Sally to tell her what was happening in her (Carol's) life. As Sally listened she became increasingly concerned that once again Carol's family members were taking advantage of her. Sally said she wanted to *help* Carol see what they were doing and to help her. But the more she tried to help, the more offended Carol became and the telephone call ended abruptly and painfully for both women.

Sally told me, "I came to your class yesterday in so much distress about this horrible phone call with my dear friend. I didn't know what I should do. All my talking and trying to clarify what I was trying to say only made things worse. It seemed like Carol's heart was so hard, and I just couldn't get through to her. I wondered if I should try another phone call, or send a gift, or even if I should fly to see her and work this out in person. I felt as though I had truly lost my best friend, and I just didn't know what to do.

"So I came to your class with all of this on my mind and heart and listened to you speak about the power of questions. I went home and thought a lot about what I had learned, and I thought about my friend and the power of questions. And then I prayed. I prayed about my friend. And I prayed to know what question I should ask that would heal her heart and our friendship.

"When I woke up this morning I knew the question I should ask. I called my friend and with all the courage I could muster and with all the love I have for her, I asked her the question. And you wouldn't believe what happened! That one question changed everything. It changed her heart. It opened and softened her heart towards me. It changed her view of me—from being a cruel meddler to truly being her dear friend. It changed our friendship. I don't think we've ever had such a heart-to-heart talk! It was a remarkable experience. That one question brought my friend back to me."

What was the question?

It was simply, *"How can I be more like you?"*

What a great question! Asking that one question healed a situation that all other efforts were only making worse!

Questions can bring remarkable healing in undeniable ways. They can bring hope.

Questions can linger on our hearts and in our minds in very useful ways, all the while inviting us to think of, and to see, things we haven't before.

Questions come with that little hook at the end. Therefore, they never come alone. They hook thoughts and feelings and possible actions. One question can pull all of that into your heart and mind. That's a pretty powerful hook! And those thoughts, feelings, and actions that are hooked work either for us or against us.

How can we use the connection between the questions we ask and the thoughts and feelings and actions that are triggered by those questions for our good?

How can we change our questions and therefore change how we think and feel about a situation and therefore change what we can do?

Solution-seeking questions

Let's start by talking about solution-seeking questions.
What kinds of questions can help you find solutions? Have you discovered some?

Think about

Take a moment to think about one question that opened your mind to a new idea when you were in the grip of an old problem.

Write about

Can you think of a time when a question helped you to "think outside the box"—that old box you had been locked up in for so long?

Think about

Think about a difficult situation you are presently in.

It's been tough slogging for a really long time, longer than you ever imagined. You continually try to make the situation better and nothing seems to change. You feel discouraged and want to cry out, as did the Prophet Joseph Smith, "Yea, O Lord, how long . . . ?" (D&C 121:3).

What happens to your mind and your heart when you "try on" the following question:

What can I do to learn from this difficult experience?

What words are you drawn to in that question?
The word *do*? The word *learn*? The word *I*?

Some useful variations on that question could be:

- **What can I do to learn what I need to learn from this difficult experience?**
- **What can I do to learn what the Lord wants me to learn from this difficult experience?**

One woman's courage, energy, and ideas started to flow when she began to use the question: *What can I do to learn from this difficult experience?* Asking that question helped her to see things she had not seen before. It was as though she had been given a new pair of glasses.

Her initial response was like the response of many others. She wrote:

"Do you mean there is something I can *do? Just that thought helps me breathe differently. When I ask myself,* 'What can I *do* to learn from this agonizing situation I am in?' *I feel as though I'm not at the bottom of a pit anymore. It almost feels as though a ladder has been given to me. I start to feel as though I can have some influence on my life and that I am not totally controlled by the situation. I like that."*

Later she wrote:

"By focusing on what I am learning through this horrible experience, I've started to think of this situation as my custom-made university course. I think I am doing post-graduate studies in life, in relationships, in me, *in prayer, in revelation. I am starting to keep notes on what I am learning and all of this is helping my thinking to shift. And that is not easy for me. But asking this question is helping and I notice that even some of my feelings are following suit. I feel less anxious. Less worried all the time. Less depressed, for sure. And I have much more energy when I ask myself, 'What can I do to learn from this difficult experience?' With the extra energy I am starting to do some things in my life other than just murmur about the situation. My old questions were zapping all my energy and I was becoming a couch potato and TV addict. I hated it. But I couldn't stop it. Or so it seemed. Yesterday I went for a walk. I called a friend I hadn't talked to in a long time. I am starting to do some things I had stopped doing. Now I find myself asking, 'Why did I stop doing those things? Why did I stop living my life just because my life wasn't what I wanted it to be?' I was in such a fog. Now, as I use the 'What can I do to learn what I need to learn from this situation' the fog is lifting. I have to use it every day. And every day I do, I see things and feel things and do things so much differently than before.*

"Maybe someone looking in at my situation would say that nothing has changed. But for me, everything is different. I am doing *and I am* learning *and I am* writing *about what I am doing and what I am learning.* ***I*** *am different."*

Think about your own personal tough situation and ask yourself:

What is it I'm supposed to be learning through this difficult situation?

That question can be so useful as we continue to discover that our timing is not the Lord's timing. When we wish that something would end, and yet it doesn't, asking the question, "What is it I'm supposed to be learning?" can help us continue to put one faith-filled footstep in front of the other. To see some things we haven't seen. To be encouraged to try some new things so we can learn what there is to learn. To pray to know what the lessons are.

Consider the question:

What is it I am supposed to be learning from this difficult situation?

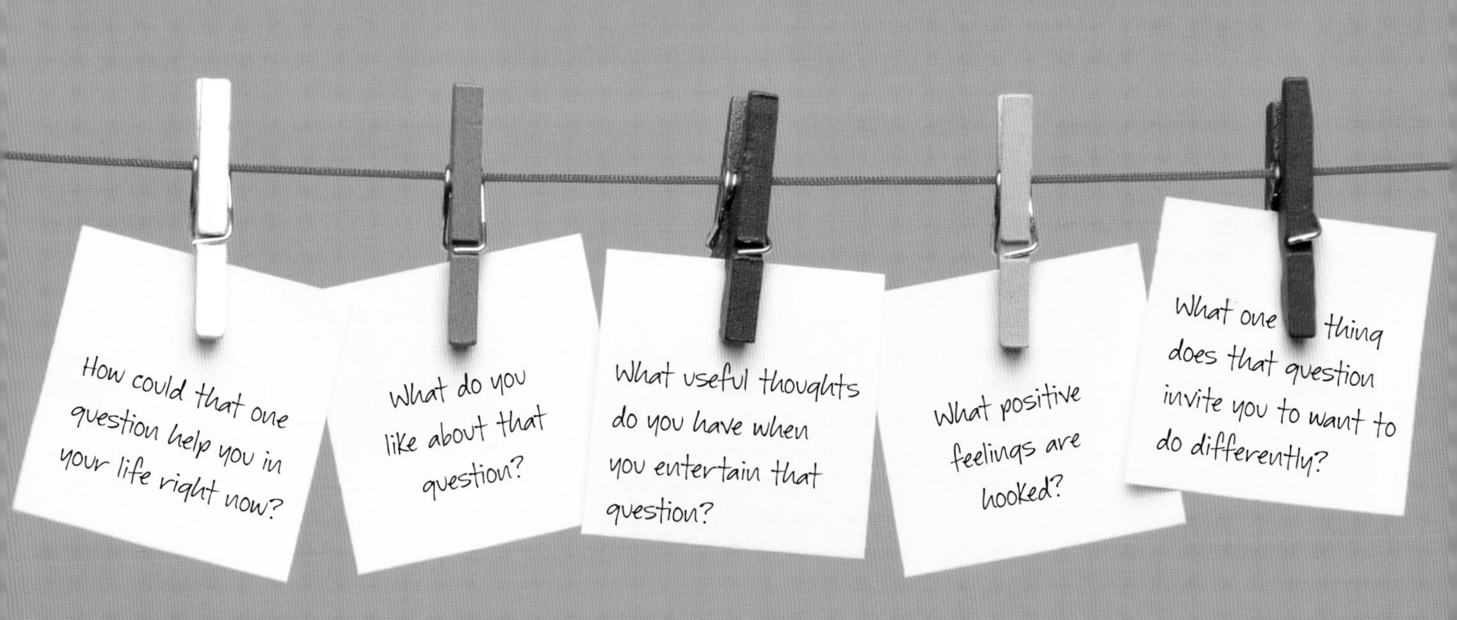

In Doctrine and Covenants 122:1–7 the Lord names more than fifteen horrendous things that could happen to the Prophet Joseph Smith, and in the end His counsel is that *"All these things shall give thee experience, and shall be for thy good"* (D&C 122:7).

Think about

Take a moment and really think about this profound promise from the Lord:

Whatever difficult situation you are in—"all these things shall give thee experience, and shall be for thy good" (D&C 122:7).

Write about

Write about three benefits that have come to your life through a very difficult experience.

This life is all about gaining experience—sometimes, perhaps most times, through experiences we would never choose on our own.

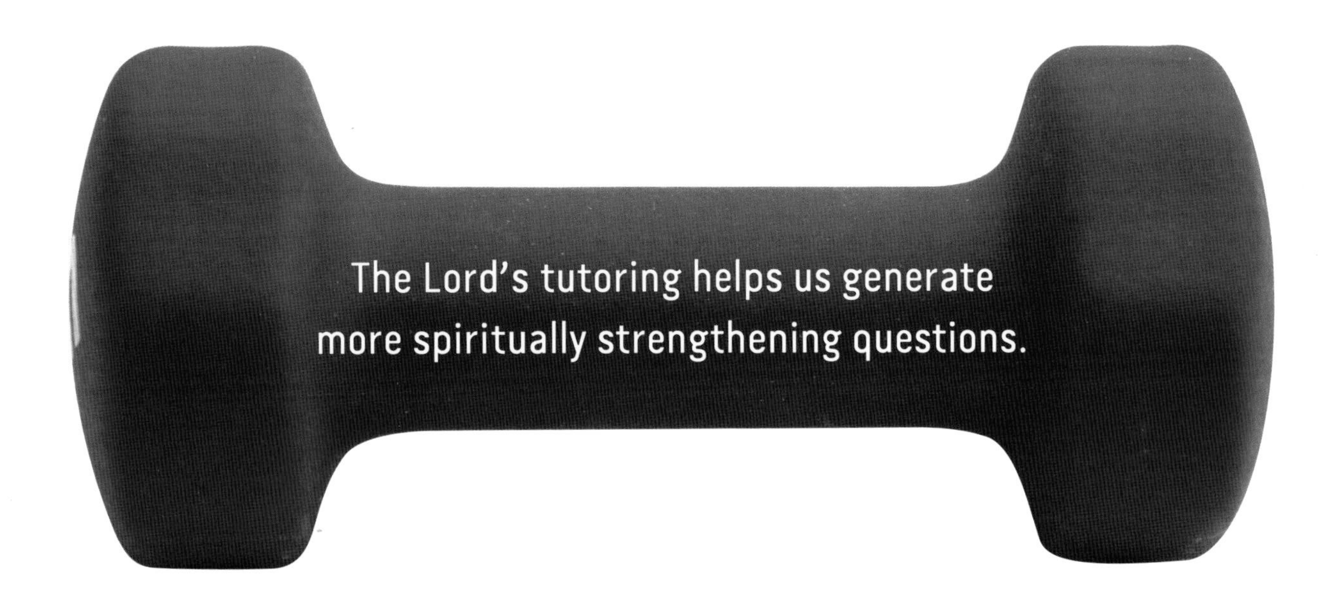

Questions such as

- How can this situation benefit me?
- What growth and new understandings will come to me out of this situation?
- How will it turn to my good?
- Has it already started to turn to my good?
- What is already happening that is good, that I have been overlooking?
- How will this situation turn to the good for those I love?
- What can I do so that this situation will turn to the good for those I love?

Think about

Consider the question

How will this situation turn to my good?

QUESTIONS CAN BE POWERFUL!

Now consider other spiritually strengthening questions that have come to your mind in the last few moments.

Write them down so you can remember them because . . .

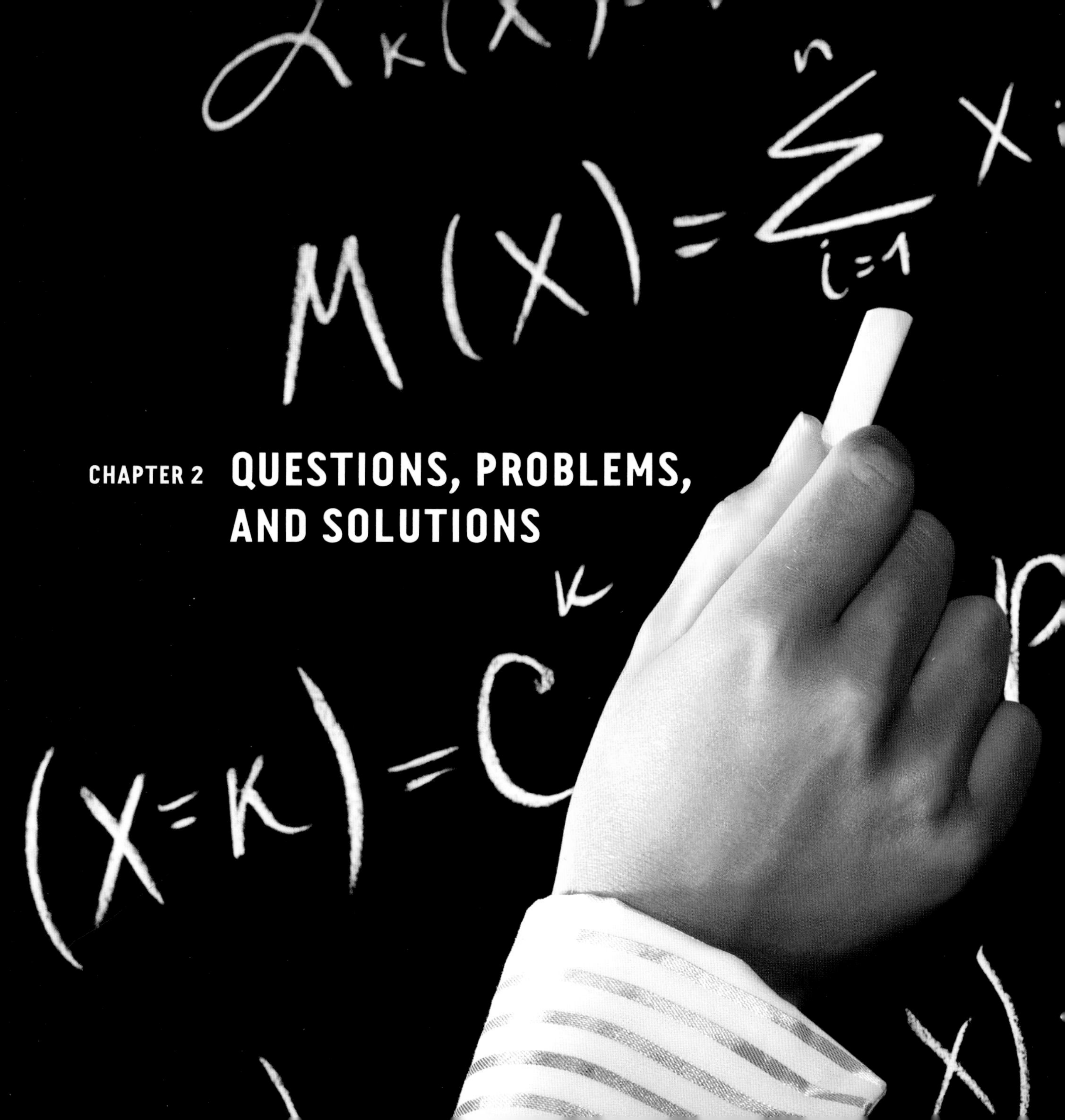

CHAPTER 2 QUESTIONS, PROBLEMS, AND SOLUTIONS

UQs & YOUR IQ

Imagine a high-tech device, newly engineered for today's world. You read the instructions, and the first thing you are to do is make an inventory of your old problems. The ones that you are weary of—bone weary. The ones that have brought you to tears and to your knees over and over again.

Next you are to select one of your most overwhelming problems and insert it into the device, which you notice is labeled UQ. You also notice that the procedure for inserting your problem into the UQ device is explained very well (and in five languages!).

You press the "Start" button and some incredible things begin to happen. Your IQ seems to increase. You suddenly feel brighter, more creative. Your view of the heart-aching situation you face begins to shift. You can see some aspects of the problem that you've overlooked, some positive aspects of yourself you've totally forgotten. People involved in the problem seem far less diabolical. You can feel some of your irritation decreasing. Some of your sadness and hurt fall away. You notice you have a bit more energy. More ideas. More courage and determination. More hope.

Could you use a UQ device in your life?

UQ stands for "Useful Question."

Learning to ask useful questions can be like owning a high-tech Useful Question device!

Asking useful kinds of questions can change our lives.

For instance, how different would your life be if instead of asking ____________ (choose one question you continually ask yourself about a persistent problem in your life), you were to ask ____________ (you will be able to fill in this blank by the end of this chapter).

The questions we ask about our problems can either help or hinder our ability to find effective solutions!

Questions can be our friends.

Questions can be great tools for solving problems.

And useful kinds of questions can solve problems and change our lives!

Think about a situation where another person's actions have caused you concern—perhaps for quite a long time.
Often in such a situation, you might ask yourself:

Why does he always . . . ?
Why doesn't she ever . . . ?
When will anyone . . . ?

Such questions have no useful answers and only bog us down.

Think about

Consider some alternative questions that can actually free your mind and heart and get you moving forward with your own life.

Focus on that same troublesome situation and ask yourself:

How is that situation a problem for me?

Why is that situation a problem for me?

Answers to these questions help uncover the real problem. Go ahead—apply them to your situation.
Can you feel some of your irritation, sadness, and frustration falling away?

Same situation.
Different questions.
Different results.

Write about

When you think about your old problem with these two questions in mind, what effect does it have on you and your troubling situation? Write about it.

IF YOU WANT TO FIND NEW SOLUTIONS,

FOUR QUESTIONS TO HELP YOU SOLVE PROBLEMS:

1. COULD YOUR SOLUTION BE THE PROBLEM?
2. COULD YOUR PROBLEM BE A SOLUTION?
3. COULD YOUR FOCUS ON THE PROBLEM BE THE PROBLEM?
4. COULD YOUR PROBLEM BE THE STORY YOU TELL ABOUT THE PROBLEM?

1. Could Your Solution Be the Problem?

How would your life change, if instead of asking:

Why doesn't anything ever change, even when I try so hard?

you were to ask:

1. *What do I usually do to try to bring about change in this troublesome situation?*
2. *Could it be that my very best efforts to solve the problem are only making the situation worse?*
3. *Could it be that my solution has now become the problem?*[1]

How would your life be different, if instead of asking:

Why does he continue to act in such an annoying, unkind, thoughtless way?

you were to ask:

1. *How do I usually respond when he acts in annoying, unkind, and thoughtless ways?*
2. *Could my response to his annoying, unkind, and thoughtless actions actually be part of the problem?*
3. *Could my response actually be inviting him to respond the way he does?*

It isn't comfortable for most of us to take responsibility for our actions at the best of times. And it's even more uncomfortable to consider that our very best efforts to *solve* a problem could actually be making a situation *worse!*

No matter what I try, nothing works! • Why doesn't anything I do make a difference? • Why does this problem seem to have a life of its own? • Why do things never change?

Is my solution to the problem now
part of the problem?
Do my best efforts actually make
the problem worse?
Has my solution now *become* the problem?

We are caught in a vicious cycle
that has no end.

In many cases it is the attempted solution to the problem that actually makes the problem worse, that contributes to the perpetuation of the problem, and that often *becomes* the problem!

Think about

Can you think of a situation where your best efforts only made the situation worse? Did your solution to the problem become the problem?

Let me give you an example. Imagine that two people are trying very hard to have a good relationship and to get along. To stay out of trouble with each other. Even to help each other. And yet the more one person nags (to solve the problem of the other person withdrawing), the more the other person withdraws (to solve the problem of the other person nagging). And the more the other person withdraws (to solve the problem of the other person nagging), the more the first person nags (to solve the problem of the other person withdrawing). And so it goes . . .

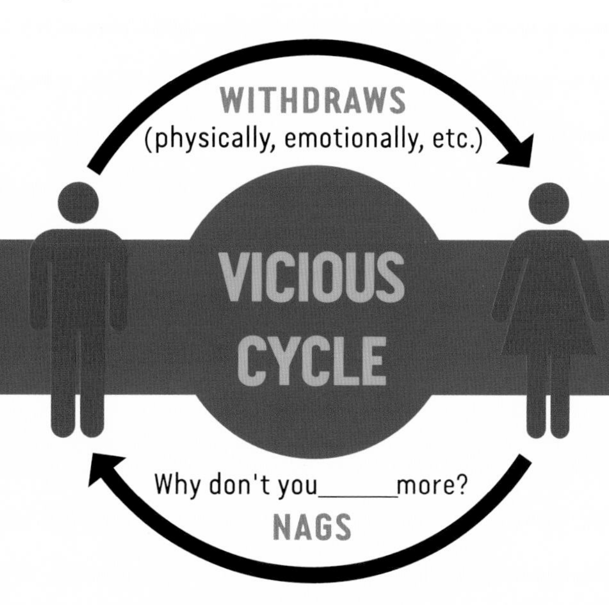

This is the classic nag-withdraw vicious cycle,[2] very common in the interactions between husbands and wives in North America. (And it is not always the wife nagging and the husband withdrawing.) The vicious cycle may be present in many different situations and may be the result of many different behaviors. When you notice a pattern beginning to develop, it would be a good time to step back and recognize your part of the cycle.

Think about

Think of a problem you have struggled with for at least six months.
Ask yourself these questions:

What have I been doing to try to solve the problem?

Could it be that my very best efforts to solve the problem are now making the situation worse?

Write about

What are your answers?

How do the questions above and your answers affect what you want to do now?

What do you see that you haven't seen before?

Write. Write. Write.

2. Could Your Problem Actually Be a Solution?

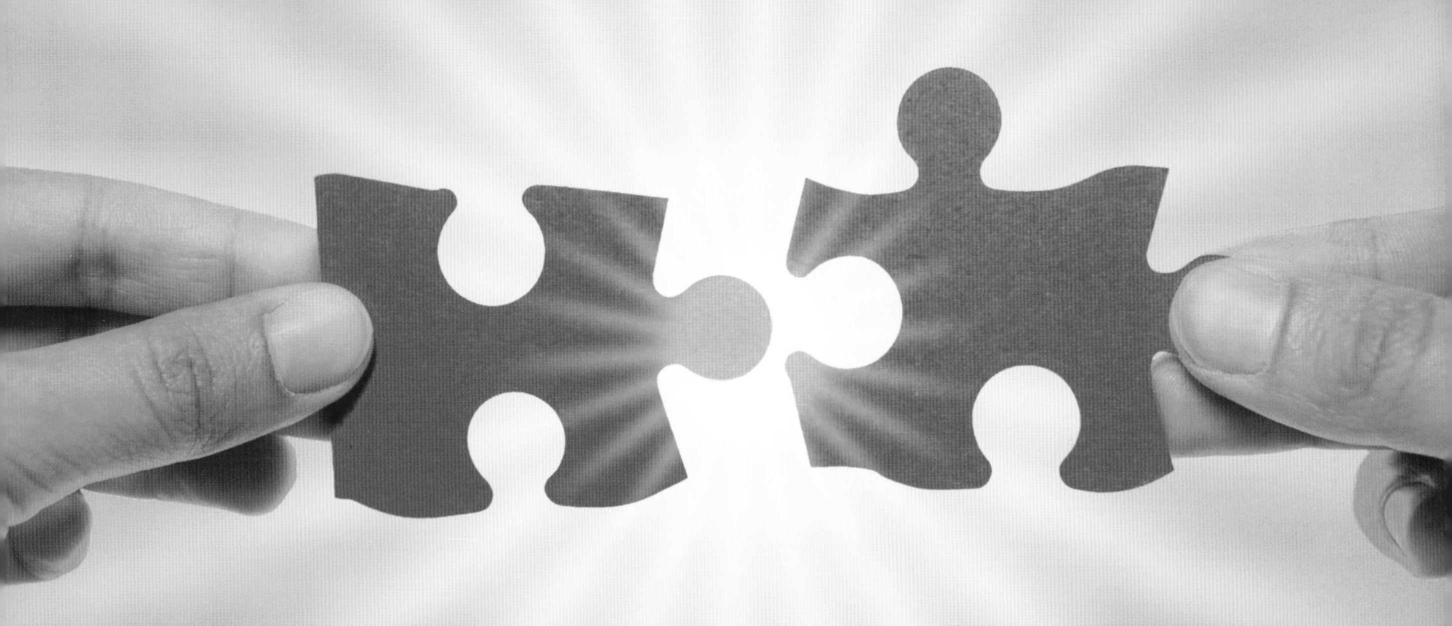

Think about

Ask yourself:

1. How different would my life be if I discovered that my problem was actually a solution to another problem?
2. To what question could my problem be an answer?

The two previous questions can help solve family problems and even problems in businesses.[3] People make tremendous progress when they use a wide-angle lens, so to speak, to consider the entire "picture" with all the people and relationships that are somehow contributing to and being affected by the problem. For example, one family member's problem may draw two other people in the family closer together.

Questions are asked such as: Who is benefiting from the problem? Which relationships are stronger because of the problem? Based upon the answers, a "prescription statement" can be offered to trigger some change. The "prescription statement" may sound like this: *Until you can find another way to* _________________ (fill in the blank with some benefit the problem is bringing to family members or their relationships), *you should continue to* _________________ (do whatever the problem behavior/thought/feeling is).

Consider the following family situation. The parents are in a heavy, heart-wrenching conflict that threatens their marriage. Their teenage son starts acting out in some manner that alarms the parents. The boy is skipping school, using drugs, coming home late. To help their son, the parents begin talking to each other, trying to find some solution. Their son's welfare becomes paramount, and the mother and father work closely with the school and other helpers to reach their son. The parents don't divorce.

Now, life is far too complicated to say that every teenager who acts out is, on a more unconscious level, trying to save his parents' relationship. Family life and relationships are far too intertwined and complex to insinuate that we should say to every trouble-making teen: *Until you can find another way to help your family, you should continue to sacrifice your own happiness and life goals and your good relationship with your parents by skipping school, using drugs, and coming home late.*

But changing our viewpoint of the problem brings to light an interesting idea that shakes up our thinking—in this case, a problem about troubled and troubling youth. Perhaps the best response to many an obstreperous teenager might be: *Thank you for helping us know that your family is in pain and needs help. Where does it hurt?*

Think about

Can you put on a wide-angle lens for a moment and look at the situation in your life that is concerning you most? Begin by thinking about all the people who are affected by your problem. Who are the people who are contributing to the problem? Zoom out with that lens as far as possible. Don't miss the people and relationships hiding in the bushes or those far out on the perimeter.

Start asking some questions:

- Could it be that my problem actually helps some people in my life?
- Could my problem be preventing some other problem?
- To what possible question in my life, or in the life of someone close to me, could my problem be an answer?

It has been said that while reading the scriptures, the Prophet Joseph Smith would try to figure out what question had been asked that led to the forthcoming of a particular passage of scripture.[4]

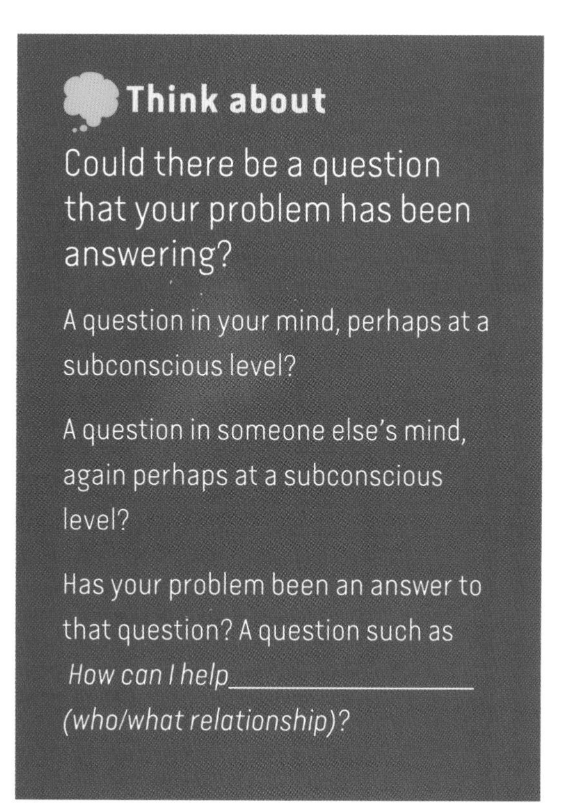

Think about

Could there be a question that your problem has been answering?

A question in your mind, perhaps at a subconscious level?

A question in someone else's mind, again perhaps at a subconscious level?

Has your problem been an answer to that question? A question such as *How can I help________________ (who/what relationship)?*

Could it be that you have been willing to sacrifice your health, your happiness, or your goals by hanging onto this problem so that someone else, or some other relationship, would benefit?

The gospel perspective, with its eternal lens and viewpoint, encourages us to look for how a difficult situation might actually be a blessing. I think of a couple struggling with the husband's cancer. After her husband's cancer had been treated, the wife said to me, "This is going to sound really strange, but I miss the rides to radiation. With cancer looming over our heads, we took time to talk. We talked about things we'd never talked about before. The cancer—which was killing my husband—actually brought our marriage to life! Now that the cancer is gone, we've gone back to our old ways."

Think about

Think of a situation in your life where the problem might actually be a solution to another problem. Ask yourself:

How does this problem **actually help** me and/or my family, friend, or colleague?

What problem might this present problem be solving—or preventing?

Write about

Write about what comes to your mind when you consider the questions on the previous page. If you can identify some benefit that is coming to someone because of your continuing problem, offer yourself the following prescription and give yourself a little jolt.

Until I can find another way to __________ (fill in the blank with what the benefit of your problem has been. For example: *help others feel good about themselves; be loyal to my father; perpetuate the memory of my mother*) **through** __________ (fill in the blank with what you have been doing. For example: *overeating; acting irresponsibly with my finances; destroying my reputation; procrastinating*)**, I should continue to sacrifice** __________ (fill in the blank with what you have been doing. For example: *my health; my happiness; my relationships*).

WHAT A WAKE-UP CALL SUCH A STATEMENT CAN BE!

And that wake-up call can lead you to ask

What is another, less destructive, more positive way that I can__________ (fill in the blank with what the benefit of your problem to yourself or others has been) **so that I can stop my problem, NOW?**

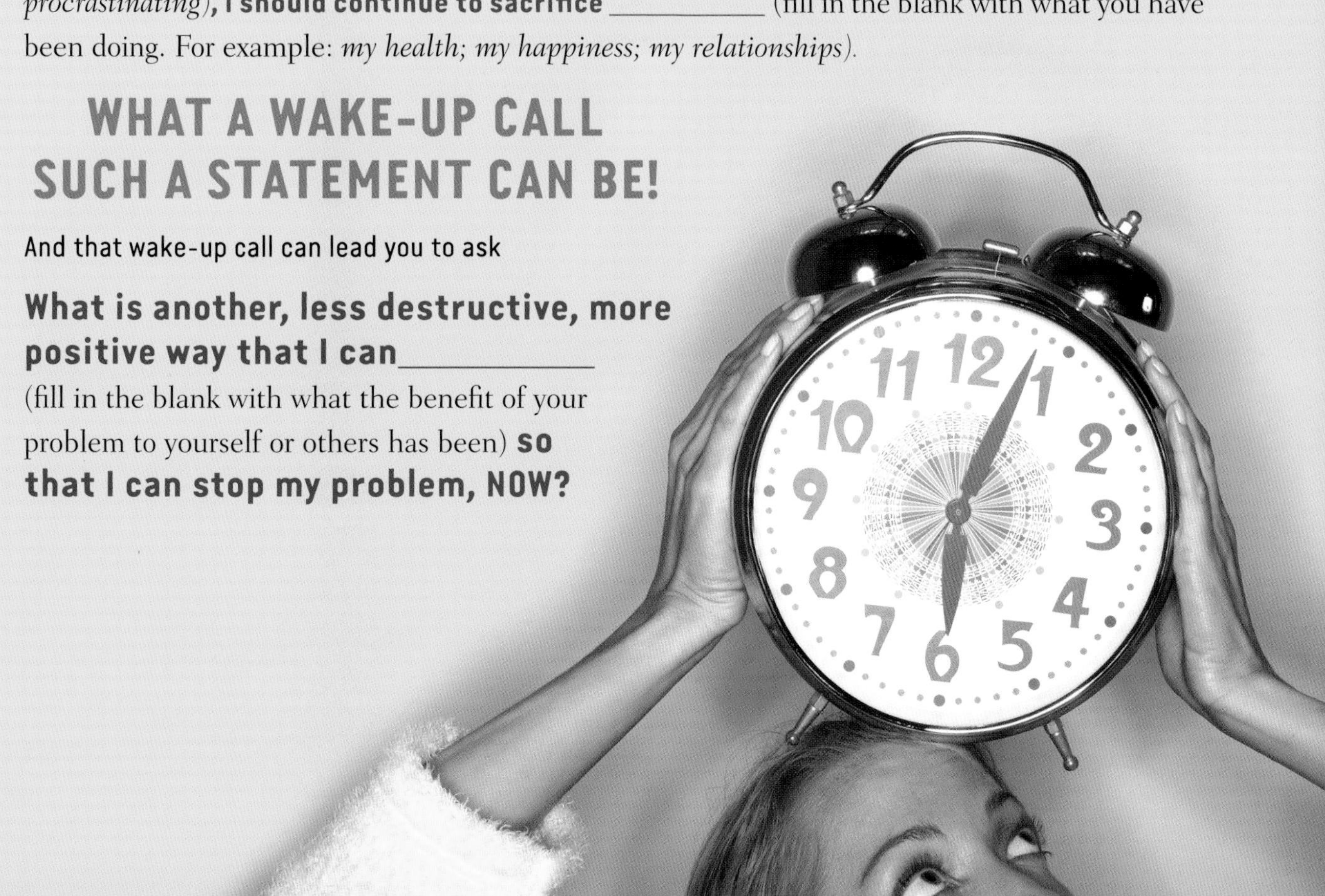

3. Could Your Focus on the Problem Be the Problem?

What is the first thing you think about when you wake up in the morning?

If the answer is "My problem," it is time for a change.

You may say, "Are you kidding? I think about my problem morning, noon, and night. And I dream about it, too." Well, all the more reason to try something different. **It's time to focus on your life without your problem.** Try it. Just for a moment.

Consider these questions:

If I woke up tomorrow and a miracle had occurred and my problem was gone,

how would I know?

what would be different?

what would I do?

What do you like about this question, called “the miracle question”?[5]

What does the miracle question invite you to want to do? To stop doing?

FOCUSING ON THE PROBLEM CAN BE THE PROBLEM

An incessant, energy-draining, idea-thwarting focus on a problem can lock people up and can become the problem.[6]

To see how this works, imagine a family where a problem has "resided" for a long time and the entire family has organized itself around the "care and keeping" of the problem.

The problem could be anything from the mother's uncontrolled diabetes to a son's struggle to keep a job and provide for his young family. All of the family's conversations—behind closed doors or face to face—focus on "the problem." The problem permeates all their interactions. It is, in fact, the center of their lives. Members of the family are defined as "good" or "bad" in relationship to how they relate to the problem. Is one family member trying to help with the problem? Is another family member to blame for the problem? Is a family member pretending there is no problem? Who in the family is able to talk about the problem without getting upset? Who takes every conversation about the problem as a personal attack?

You get the picture. Most of us are familiar with what happens when a problem becomes the focus of our lives.

Now you try it.

Think of your situation and ask yourself the miracle question:

If I woke up tomorrow and a miracle had occurred and my problem was gone,

- how would I know?
- what would be different?
- what would I do?

Write about

Take a few minutes to write down your answers. Also write about other thoughts that come to you as you consider your life without the problem.

How will your life be different without the problem?

Without the problem to consume you, how would you feel?

What might you be able to accomplish if the problem were to go away?

4. Could Your Problem Be the Story You Tell about the Problem?

Imagine if a movie director approached you and said, "I would like to make a movie of your life. You can tell the story of your life any way you would like. It's your story to tell. We just need to know if you would like to be cast as a victim, a survivor, or a hero in the movie of your life." What would you say? How would you answer?

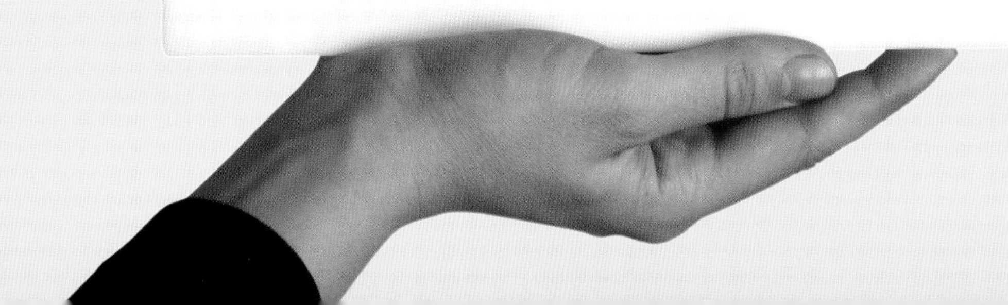

Victim? Survivor? Hero?

What story have you been telling yourself and others about you and your life?[7] How have you been casting yourself? As the story of your life unfolds, each time you tell someone how you are doing or what you are doing, do you emerge as victim, survivor, or hero?

How should we define *victims, survivors,* and *heroes?*

VICTIMS–those who are downtrodden and are always under the influence of someone or some problem or force. One can be a victim even of time and "busyness."

SURVIVORS–those who seek constantly to find a way just to stay afloat amid unending difficulties, challenges, and disasters.

HEROES–those who have discovered the strength, skills, and understanding to enjoy a rich, full life—despite horrific problems they never thought they would be battling and that would defeat a lesser person. A hero is also keen to help others by sharing what they have discovered.

The gospel teaches that each of us was born to be a hero! We were born to succeed. With the Lord's help, the hero that you truly are can and will emerge!

Think about

... the following questions:

- If you have always thought of yourself as a victim because of hideous things that have happened to you, can you see anything that tells you that you are actually a survivor?
- What would you need to do, or recognize that you have already done, so that you would cast yourself as a hero?

Same troublesome, even terrifying, situation but with a different response from you. A heroic response!

- Can you think of one instance where you were prepared to respond to the old troublesome situation as a victim and instead you responded as a survivor, or even a hero?
- Which of the following introductions would be most accurate in describing your life story?

  This is the story of someone who had the courage to ...

  This is the story of someone who wished she had had the courage to ...

  This is the story of someone who realized just in time that she had the courage to ...

Positive changes are more likely to occur in a person's life when that person:

1. Has a bright recollection of times in her life when she handled something well. She is able to recall those times when she was almost tempted to respond in the old victim mode, but didn't!

2. Is able to think and talk about his problems as being outside of himself, rather than something that defines who he is.

3. Sees herself as one who has risen above obstacles, conquered difficulties, and has been able to wrestle problems to the ground—someone who has been honed by, instead of overwhelmed by, the challenges she has faced. Her life story is not a "problem-saturated story" but rather a story of a survivor, even a hero![8]

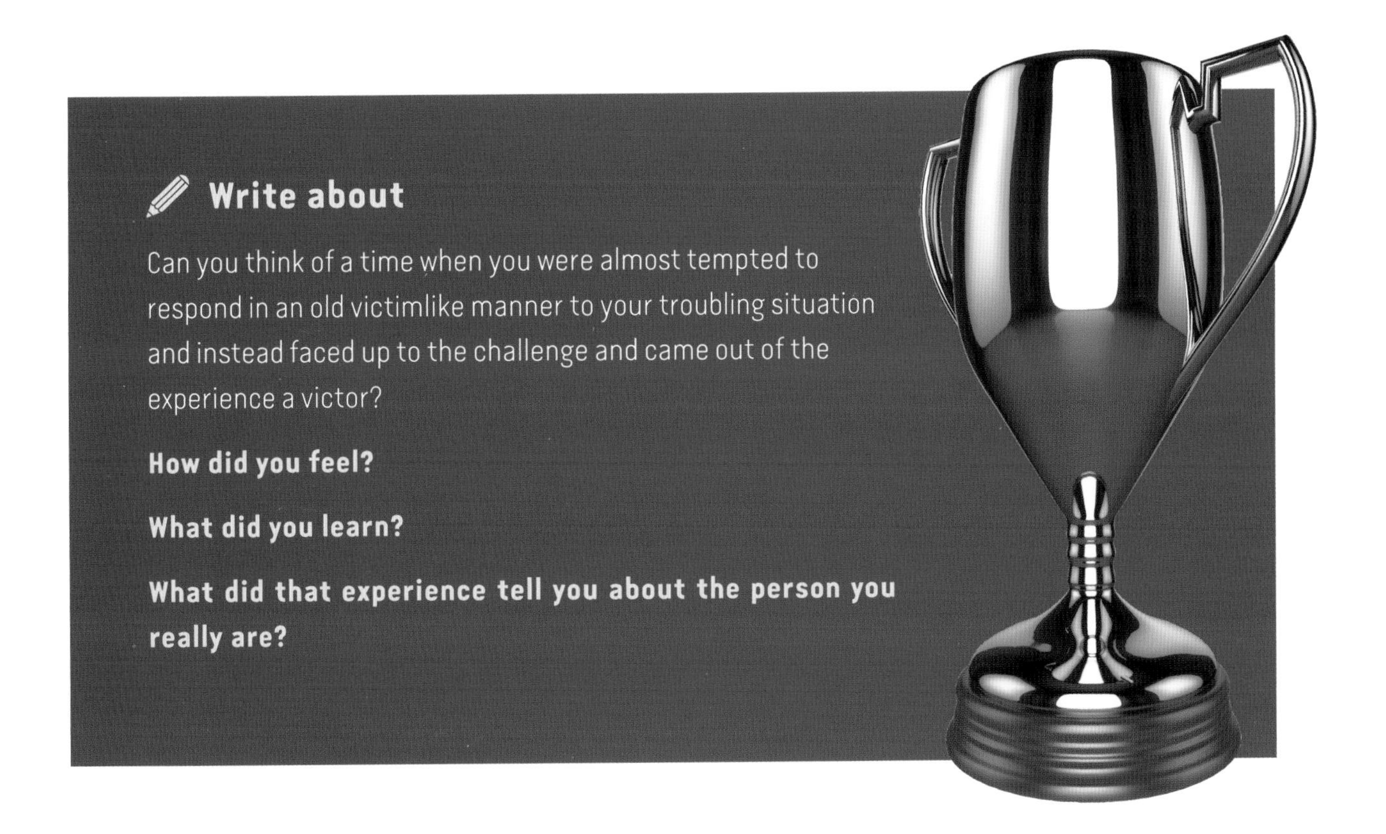

Write about

Can you think of a time when you were almost tempted to respond in an old victimlike manner to your troubling situation and instead faced up to the challenge and came out of the experience a victor?

How did you feel?

What did you learn?

What did that experience tell you about the person you really are?

Think about

Picture your problem as an actual entity—a thing, something that you could place on a table, or seat in a chair. An object that you can clearly see is outside of you. If your problem is *loneliness*, picture putting loneliness in a chair. Notice how big it is. What it looks like. Give it size, shape, color, texture. Perhaps even a name.

Imagine the conversation you could have with loneliness if you could see it for what it really is—some *thing* that is trying to get you off your life-path, to discourage you, to distract you. What might you want to say to loneliness now that you can see it, not as some character flaw, but as an entity outside of yourself?

Write about

To help you with your conversation with your problem (loneliness, fear, etc.) perhaps these writing prompts can help.

Dear (the name of your problem):

Actually (name of problem), I don't want to call you "Dear" because you have hurt me so much.

You entered my life

You have influenced me by

You have made me doubt

You have whispered lies to me, like

You have made me

You have affected my family by

You have affected my relationships with others by

I want you to know that, although I had nothing to do with you initially forcing your way into my life, I am coming to understand that I have unintentionally invited you to stay in my life by

I now understand that some of the things that made me vulnerable to keeping you and your influence in my life were

I can now see that some of my greatest strengths and resources in overcoming you and your effects on my life are

When I am free from you and your influence, ______ and ______ will replace you, and I will feel

And look

And love

One time when you tried to rule me but I was able to be stronger than you was

As trying as "our relationship" has been over the years, you, (name of your problem), and your effects have taught me, and are teaching me

In closing I would like to say

Write about

Write the story of your life with you as hero! Same facts. Different story. This one features you rising above obstacles, conquering difficulties, wrestling problems to the ground. In short, arising as a hero in the midst of the same troubling circumstances that used to make you think of yourself as a victim.

Take time to do this exercise and see what you discover about yourself. See what you are drawn to do when you think of yourself and write about yourself as the hero in your life story. After all, it is *your* life story, and you are writing pages of it every day.

Take your time with this writing adventure. You might want to set it aside for a while (perhaps a day or two), then go back and read it and see what you discover.

Try it

Try writing the next week of your life in advance. What hero-like things will you do, say, think, and feel in order to live a hero's life this very next week?

ASKING USEFUL KINDS OF QUESTIONS CAN CHANGE OUR LIVES

Which of the four questions we discussed will help you the most?

- Could your solution be the problem?
- Could your problem be a solution?
- Could your focus on the problem be the problem?
- Could your problem be the story you tell about the problem?

And now, how would you fill in the blanks of the question asked at the beginning of this chapter:

How different would your life be if instead of asking ________ (what question did you write at the beginning of this chapter?), you were to ask ________?

Let's say it even more positively:

My life will be different from this moment on because I am going to stop asking ______ (your old question) and start asking ______ (a new question based on what you learned in this chapter).

CHANGE YOUR QUESTIONS CHANGE YOUR LIFE!

CHAPTER 3 THREE KINDS OF QUESTIONS

Let me introduce you to three kinds of questions that can increase our ability to see that which we have not been able to see previously.[1] These kinds of questions can change our conversations with others, dramatically change our understanding of others, and even change their understanding of themselves.

These three kinds of questions can gather information and introduce information simultaneously. That's what makes them so effective.

I remember teaching student nurses who were concerned that they had so little time to find out how their patients were really feeling. Learning to ask these kinds of questions was key to meeting the nurses' time constraints. Any one of these questions could be considered a "nursing intervention" and help patients heal.

The three kinds of questions are

Difference Questions

Behavioral Effect Questions

and

What If Questions

LET'S START WITH *DIFFERENCE QUESTIONS.*

Difference questions are based upon the idea that difference is information.[2]

Difference IS information.

We know that something is *cold* because something else is *hot*.
We know that something is *hard* because something else is *soft*.
Think of all the differences that can be explored.
Difference is information.

Difference Questions

- Explore differences between people, relationships, and situations.
- Use words such as "most," "least," "best," "worst," "biggest," or "smallest."

Let's consider some examples.

To a daughter whose father has just been diagnosed with Alzheimer's disease, a helpful difference question might be

Are you ***more*** *concerned about* ***your mom or your dad*** *since your father was diagnosed with Alzheimer's?*

Think about

What difference is being explored with that question?

You're right: the difference between people, i.e. the daughter's concern about her mother versus her father at this crucial time of the diagnosis of Alzheimer's.

Now, that question might not just gather information, it may also introduce *new* information. The question might help the daughter think about something she hasn't yet considered. For example, with all the upheaval surrounding her father's diagnosis, the daughter may have been so focused on her father that she may have forgotten entirely about what might be happening with her mother as a result of the diagnosis. As soon as the question is asked—*Are you* ***more concerned about your mom or your dad*** *since your father was diagnosed with Alzheimers?*—the daughter may ask herself the additional question:

"What is concerning me *the most* about Dad?" That particular difference question can be very helpful as the daughter tries to rank her concerns and therefore know where she should put her energy and time right now.

Then the daughter may think, *Well, I can't even answer the question about who I am more concerned about until I think for a moment about Mom. What is happening to her through all of this? What do I need to start noticing about my mother so I can help her? What questions can I ask her so I can find out what is concerning her the most?*

Can you see how asking just one question can trigger some great thinking and conversations? And not just between you and the daughter (that may be the least important), but between the daughter and her mother, the daughter and her father, the mother and father, and within the daughter. The ripple effect of asking that one question can be far-reaching and so much more useful than a typical question one might ask the daughter such as, "What are you concerned about with your dad, now that he has been diagnosed with Alzheimer's?"

The daughter, so overwhelmed with everything, may think to herself, *I don't even know where to start. And I don't have time to tell you everything I am concerned about.*

Again, can you see the wisdom in asking a difference question such as, "What is concerning you **the most at this time**?" Such a question not only focuses the mind but also puts a time frame on it. Two very useful things to do in a time of crisis.

Another benefit of asking a difference question is that whether a person answers the question at the time or not, the question often lingers. Difference questions have an unusual "staying power," so the thoughts and feelings and actions the question triggers can influence the situation even when you are not present.

Can you see why asking these kinds of questions can be so effective?

These questions introduce new ideas. They introduce change.

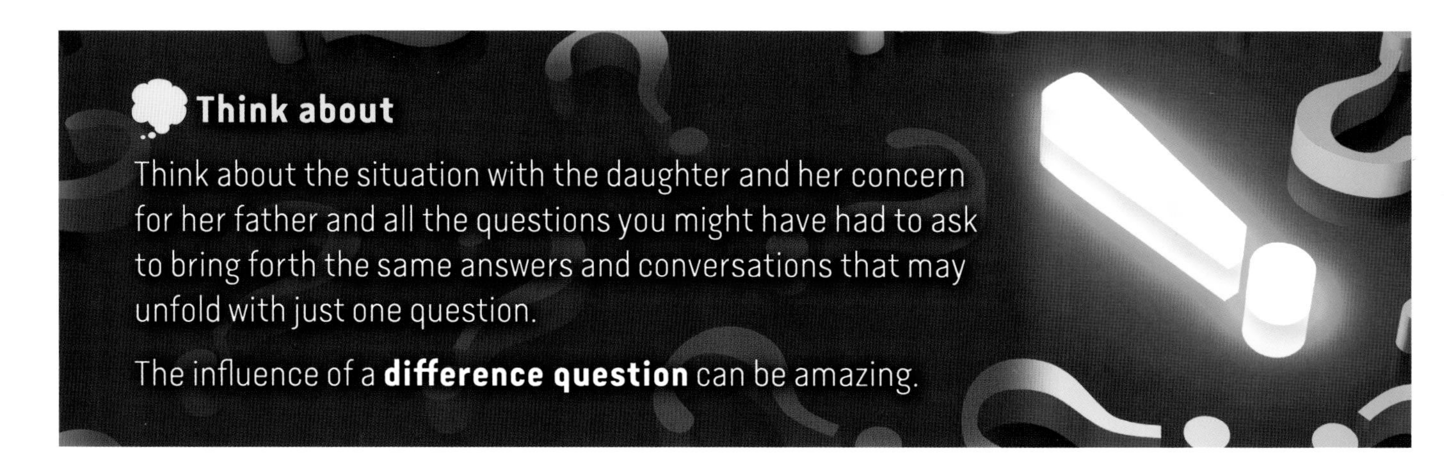

Think about

Think about the situation with the daughter and her concern for her father and all the questions you might have had to ask to bring forth the same answers and conversations that may unfold with just one question.

The influence of a **difference question** can be amazing.

Write about

Are you willing to take a chance?

You may think it's premature, but try writing a difference question that would help you with your present situation. Perhaps a difference question would help you connect more closely with someone you love. Use the word "most" or "least."

Let's consider another situation and another difference question:

A woman you know is just entering the empty-nest phase of her life, and you have noticed her sadness. Instead of merely asking her what's wrong, you may want to ask her:

*What is **the biggest difference** since your last child left home?*

What is the effect of this question? It allows your friend to explore the difference between two situations: her life with children in her home and her life without.

You've just thrown a pebble into her huge pool of sadness with that question. The woman is invited to look at her life and sift through the changes that have recently occurred. She can review in her mind how things were with her children present and how things are now that they have moved on. She may see that some things haven't changed all that much, and that other things have changed tremendously. She can then sort through the differences and see which one she would select as the *biggest* difference.

All of this thinking and sorting can be helpful, even healing. And through the process she may even begin to see that some of the changes aren't all bad—and some may even "turn to her good" (D&C 51:17)!

Let's think about another situation and a difference question that would help someone explore a change in relationships:

A friend's mother has recently slipped through the veil. It may be useful to ask her:

Now that your mother has died, do you think that your relationship with your father or your relationship with your sister will change more?

How might that question be helpful in stimulating additional conversation and even promote healing?

Considering such a question can invite your friend to think about the possibility of other changes that may follow her mother's death. It may prompt your friend to do things that will draw her closer to her sister and her father. Even if the woman's response to the question is "I don't know," the difference question can percolate, inviting her to think about and do things she may not have otherwise thought or done. Asking a useful difference question can be a gift that keeps on giving.

Think about

Think about the difference a difference question can make in the following example:

A young woman is dating and wants to understand if her prospective husband is under the influence of pornography. The question "Do you have a problem with pornography?" is not a very useful question to ask, because most people, if not all people, with a pornography problem think they don't have one. But imagine the conversation that could unfold if she were to ask her boyfriend, "*What is the* ***most effective*** *thing you do to keep yourself safe from the pornographic images that pop up on your computer, TV, or cell phone?*"

Now consider these difference questions. How could they help you? What do they invite you to think about, feel, or do differently?

What is the biggest misconception my spouse (or child, friend, sibling) has about me? What might be the most helpful thing I could do to change that misconception?

What do I do that helps my spouse (or child, friend, parent) feel the most loved?

Now that is an invitation to reflection! Consider all we are invited to think about in order to answer that one difference question.

Write about

Write your answers to those difference questions.

Write the questions you had to ask yourself in order to answer those difference questions.

Difference questions really work.

They are effective.

They are efficient.

They can help get to the heart of a matter, and they can introduce helpful, healing ideas into people's hearts and minds.

They can help us speak the unspeakable, which can be healing in and of itself.

Think of a situation that is concerning you.

Write a difference question that will explore
a difference between two people,
two relationships,
two situations,
or two ideas.

Write about

Think of how useful difference questions could be in the process of getting to know someone.

Try to write a difference question that would help you love someone you already love even more.

Make it easy and use words such as *most*, *least*, *biggest*, and *smallest* to help you.

What difference question would allow someone to get to know *you* better?

THE SECOND KIND OF QUESTION IS CALLED A *BEHAVIORAL EFFECT QUESTION.*

Just as the name suggests, behavioral effect questions explore the effect of one's behavior on thoughts and feelings and other behaviors.

Consider these examples of how behavioral effect questions can be useful.

If you are present when a husband is hesitant to reach out to his wife, who is crying, you could ask a behavioral effect question. Rather than say to the husband, "Please reach out and comfort your wife," you might ask him instead:

When you see your wife weeping, what is that like for you?

What does her weeping make you want to do?

That particular behavioral effect question invites the husband to explore the effect of his wife's behavior (her weeping) on his thoughts, feelings, and actions and allows him to behave of his own volition.

Asking that question is almost always helpful, as ninety-nine times out of a hundred, the husband will answer, "It makes me want to reach out to her." And most of them follow by spontaneously reaching out and comforting the crying wife. Sometimes a husband may say, "I want to reach out and comfort her, but I am afraid she'll reject me." Or "I don't know how." Those responses can also be helpful and can begin a healing conversation for the couple.

Here is another example of how a behavioral effect question can be useful.

To a friend whose son has not been coming home on time, you may want to ask:

When your son comes home late, what thoughts do you have?

This simple question can invite your friend to explore the effect her son's behavior has on her thoughts. For example, does she tell herself that she is a bad mother? That she is losing her son? What fears arise in her mind? What catastrophic expectations does she already have? All of that can be explored by having her respond to just one question.

Write about

Write one behavioral effect question. Remember, you are exploring the effect that someone's behavior has on another person's thoughts, feelings, or actions. Do you notice that even simply thinking about and writing down the behavioral effect question increases your understanding of, or empathy for, the situation?

A behavioral effect question can also be posed to explore the effect of someone's behavior on his own thoughts, feelings, and actions.

For example, here is a behavioral effect question that might be asked of a person who is stuck in a self-defeating vicious cycle of irresponsible eating and weight gain:

When you find yourself eating in a manner that guarantees you will gain weight, just after you have made a pledge to eat healthily, what do you tell yourself? How do you feel? What do you do then?

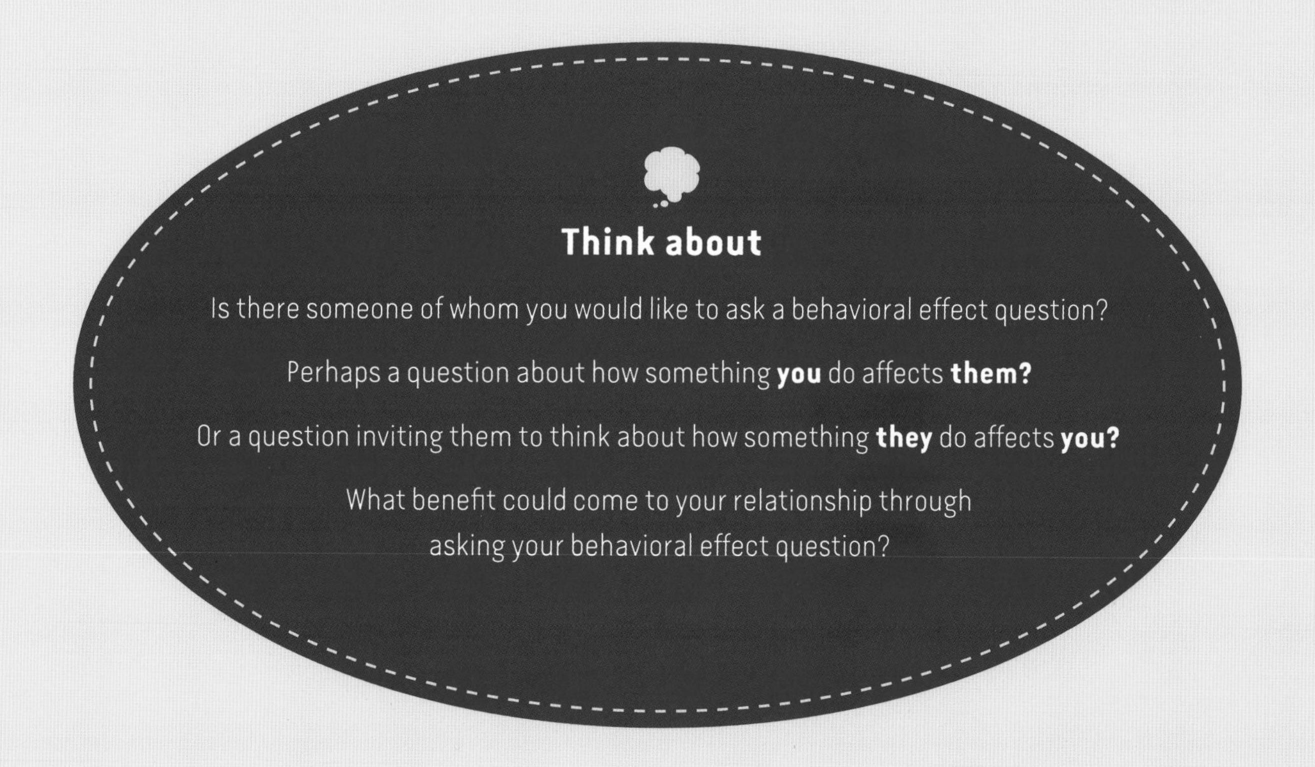

Think about

Is there someone of whom you would like to ask a behavioral effect question?

Perhaps a question about how something **you** do affects **them?**

Or a question inviting them to think about how something **they** do affects **you?**

What benefit could come to your relationship through asking your behavioral effect question?

THE THIRD KIND OF QUESTION IS CALLED A *WHAT IF QUESTION.*

The clinical name is the "hypothetical/future-oriented" question, but we're going to just call it a what if question. The what if question invites exploration of possibilities, alternative actions, or meanings. What if questions invite us to think of things that haven't happened yet, but could.

A fascinating story is told about the effect of just one what if question.[3] A therapist was interviewing several adult children in a family where the mother was gravely ill. All the adult children spoke very disparagingly about their father, who was not present. They portrayed him as a deadbeat dad and one in whom there was nothing to admire. The tone of the conversation shifted dramatically, however, and the pejorative view of the father turned into a compassionate and caring view when the therapist asked one what if question:

If your mother were to die, what would your father do?

Let's consider some other examples.

To a woman whose husband has lost his job, a what if question might be:

If your husband were to find a job tomorrow, is there anything about that situation that would concern you?

This is an unexpected question, as most women would be happy to have their husbands find new employment. But perhaps there are some things—about the new job or about having her husband away after enjoying him being at home—that would be useful for this woman to think about and acknowledge.

Or you might ask:

If your husband were never to find a job for the rest of his life, how would the two of you manage?

It can be useful to invite people to think of alternative outcomes of a situation. Also, when someone is so certain that a particular action means one thing, helping them to consider another view of the situation can open their mind to another possible meaning for the very same behavior and can be helpful.

Of a mother who is having trouble letting go of her daughter, you might ask:

If you thought that your daughter's not calling you the other night meant that you had raised her well and she was feeling responsible and confident living away from you—rather than that she doesn't love you anymore—what would you do? How would you respond to encourage her confidence in herself and in her relationship with the Lord?

Think about

Think about a troublesome situation in your life.

Now, play with various aspects of the situation by asking yourself such what if questions as:

"What if such and such were the case instead of how it is?"

Turn the whole situation upside down. Suspend reality for a moment and see what new ideas present themselves.

"What if the timing were different?"

What if all of this were happening one year from now—or five or ten years from now—instead of right now? What difference would that make?

"What if the people involved were different?"

What if Mom had been diagnosed with Alzheimer's instead of Dad? How would that change things?

"What if the actions taken were different?"

What would happen if instead of trying to keep my pain a secret I could tell a confidante? Would that make a difference?

Write about

After thinking about your situation, write one what if question.

What one thing does that question invite you to want to do or to do differently?

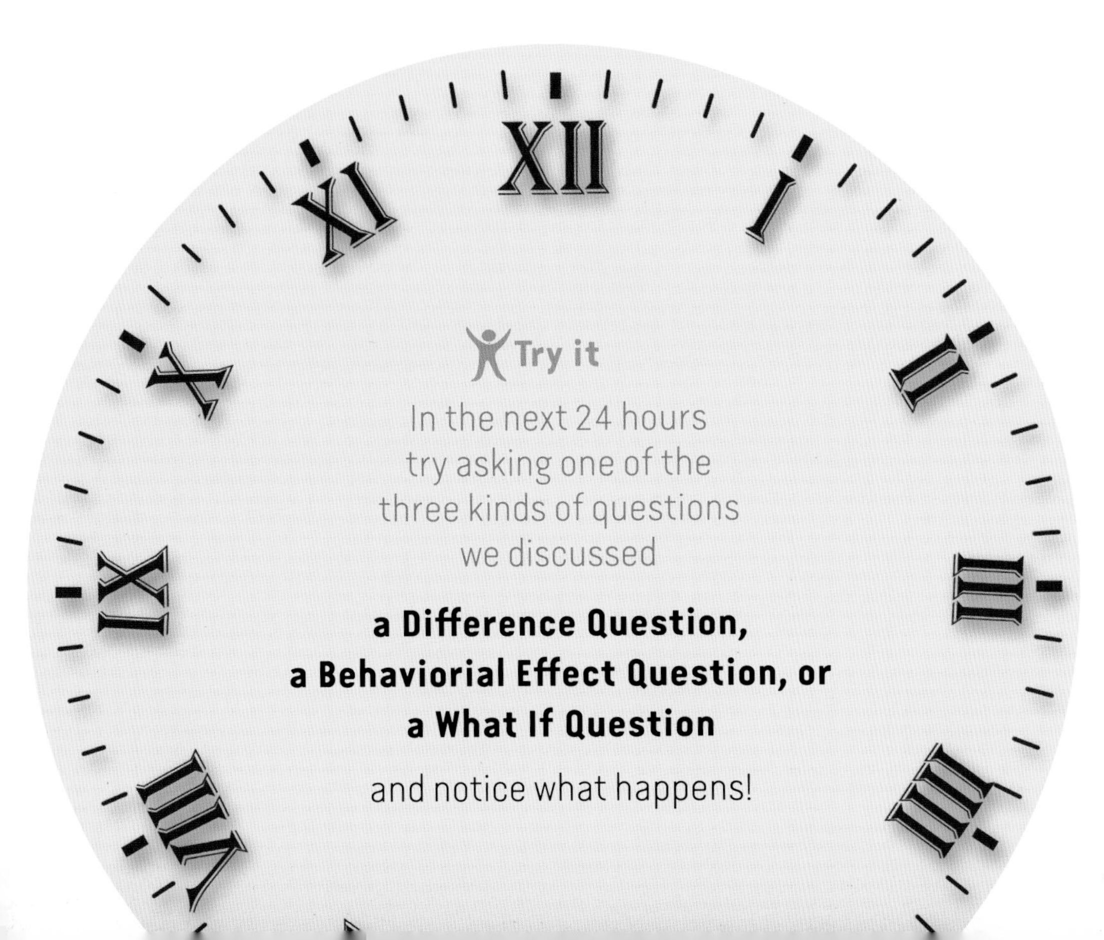

Try it

In the next 24 hours try asking one of the three kinds of questions we discussed

a Difference Question,
a Behaviorial Effect Question, or
a What If Question

and notice what happens!

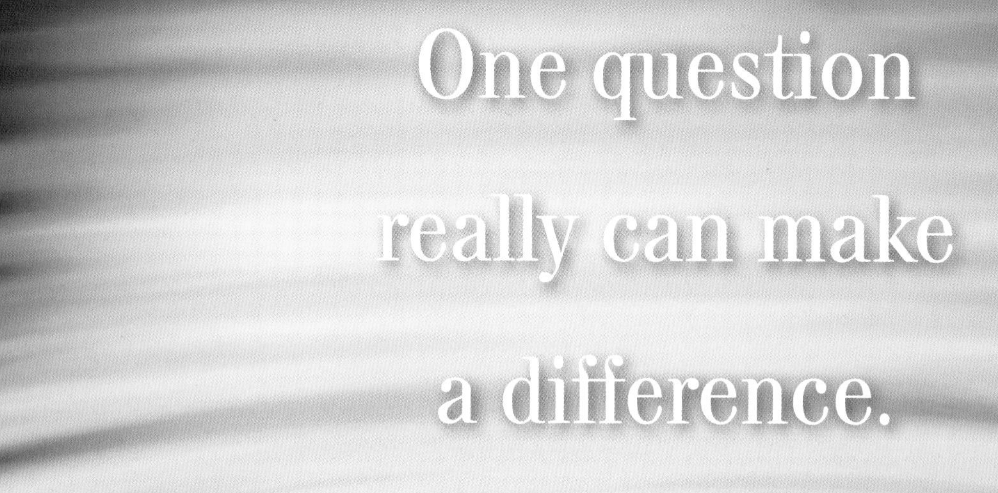
One question
really can make
a difference.

CHAPTER 4 BELIEFS AND QUESTIONS

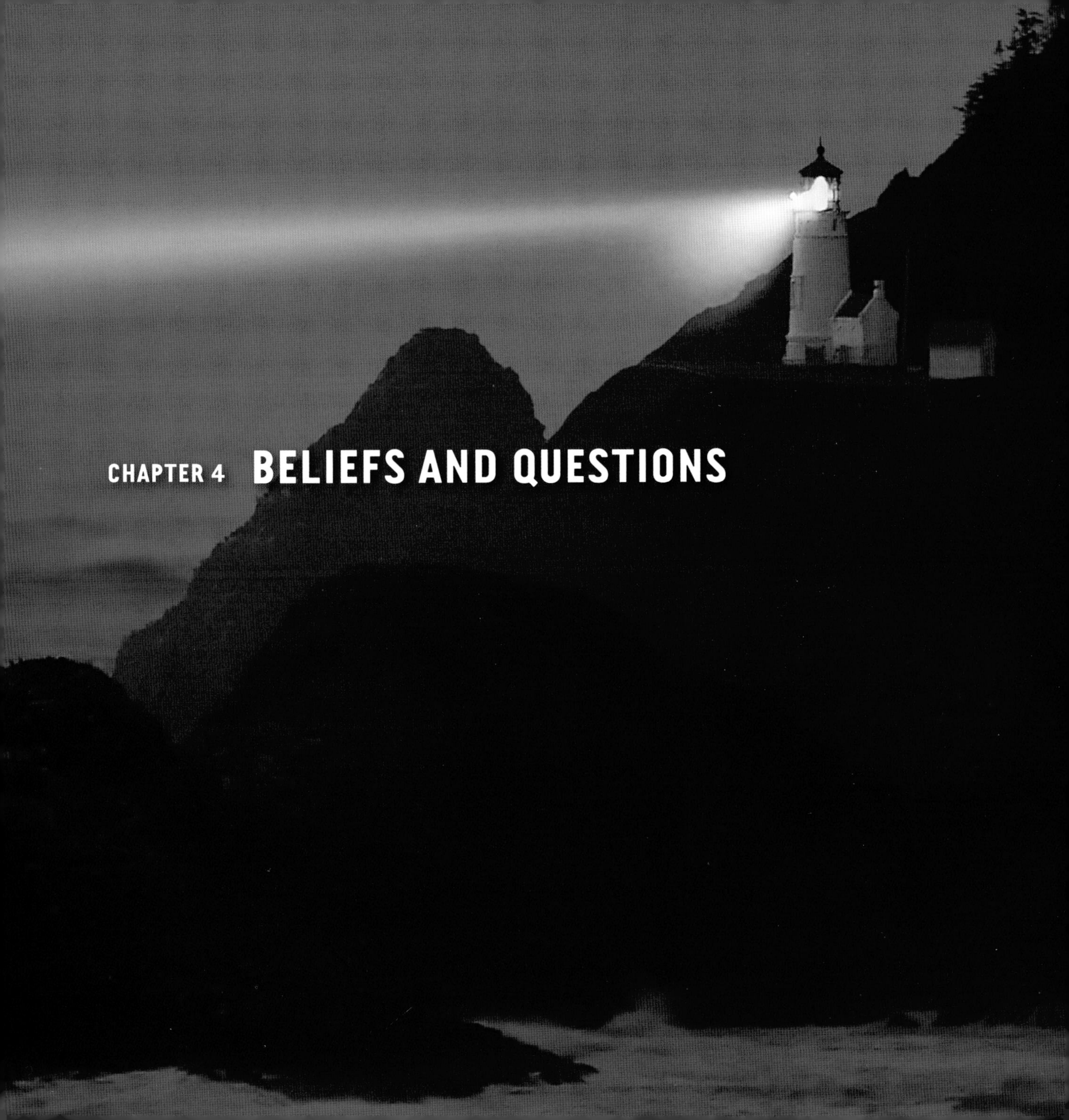

COULD YOUR BELIEFS BE THE PROBLEM?

Your beliefs influence everything you see, think, feel, and do. Some of your beliefs are helpful and some are not! Some beliefs can promote solutions; some, problems. What are your beliefs doing for you?[1]

Let's start with the definition of a belief. A belief is the lens through which we view the world.[2] With that definition in mind, it follows that:

Believing Is Seeing!

Yes, our beliefs influence what we are able to see. What else influences what we see in the world around us? Answer:

The state of our physical, psychological, social, and spiritual self influences what we are presently able to see.

For instance, if we are tired, feeling mistreated, lonely, or spiritually bankrupt, we may not see things the same way we would if we were rested; feeling loved, supported, needed, and wanted; and were spiritually in tune with the Lord.

We see things as WE really are!

Do you remember the question that the angel asks Nephi when he shows Nephi the tree of life? He asks, *"What beholdest thou?"* (1 Nephi 11:14). I wonder if the angel was merely asking: *"What do you see?"* Or could it be that he was trying to determine, *"What are you able to see?"* What Nephi was able to see would reveal his current spiritual capacity.

The truth is that painful or confusing life experiences can distort our way of looking at things and generate beliefs that constrain us and cause problems.

We may see things that aren't there, and we may not see things that are!

If what we believe has been derived through a warped or fractured lens and we aren't seeing things as they really are, it becomes difficult to reach useful conclusions or make good decisions.

One key to solving our problems is to identify the beliefs that are at the heart of the matter—our core beliefs.

There are two kinds of core beliefs:

- Hindering or constraining beliefs, which decrease options for solutions
- Helpful or facilitating beliefs, which increase options for solutions

Hindering or constraining beliefs lock us up.
They lock up our minds and our hearts.
They lock up our solution-seeking and
problem-solving abilities.
Constraining beliefs hold our true selves captive!
On the other hand . . .

Helpful or facilitating beliefs free our minds and hearts and help us see situations with new eyes and greater energy. Our vision, our thoughts, our feelings are not restricted or constrained. We feel as though we can see forever.

Helpful or facilitating beliefs keep us open to divine truths and direction.

Ways to Discover Your Core Beliefs

Your core beliefs are revealed in the questions you ask yourself and in the stories you tell. Let me walk you through some experiences that will help you uncover your beliefs by looking at key questions and important stories in your life.

Think about

What questions do you ask yourself

when things go wrong, when people disappoint you, when troubles and tragedies happen, when you are having a really bad day?

Go back in your mind. Do you say to yourself, "Why can't I ever get a break?" Or perhaps, "Why me?"

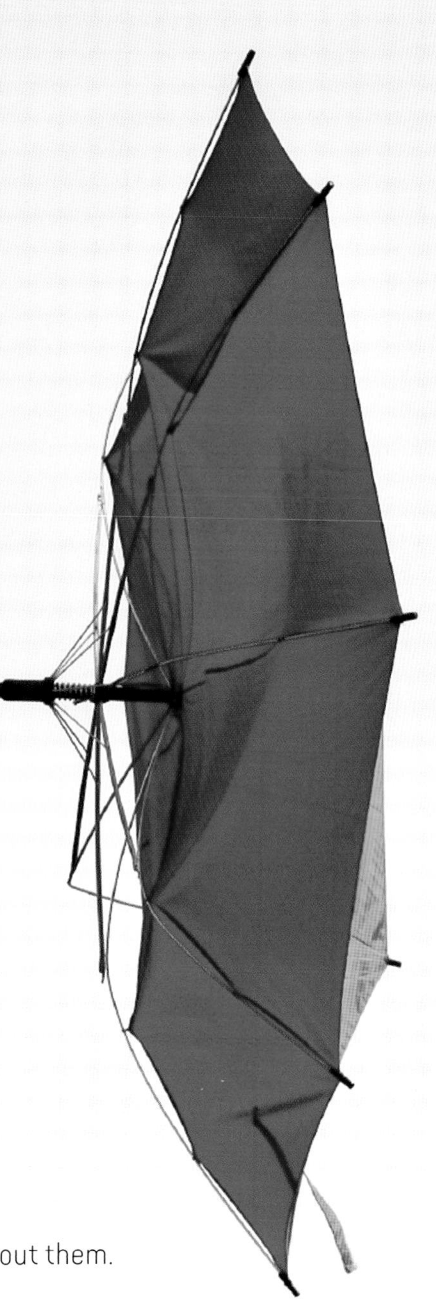

Write about

Write the questions you ask yourself whenever lousy, terrible, horrific things happen to you.

Put them down on paper so you can see them. Now, looking at those questions, can you see some hints about what you believe about life? love? yourself? others? the Lord?

Really think about the questions and your beliefs. Now write about them.

Think about

Now think of the questions you ask yourself on a good day.

Go back in your mind. What questions do you ask yourself when things go well, when people are kind to and appreciative of you, when successes occur? Do you say, “Why am I so blessed or lucky?” or “What horrible thing is going to happen now that this good thing has occurred?”

Write about

Write down the questions you ask yourself on a good day so you can see them.

Looking at those questions, can you see some hints about what you believe about life? love? yourself? others? the Lord?

Really think about the questions and your beliefs. Write about them.

Now review what you have written. Would you say your beliefs are “helpful and facilitating” or “hindering and constraining”?

Let's try another approach to uncover some of your core beliefs.

Think of a family motto that influenced your life as you grew up, a theme that guided how family members behaved. Perhaps it was an official family motto or maybe it was an "unofficial" motto that you learned as you observed your parents living their lives.

Do any of the following sound familiar?

"Big boys don't cry."

"It's always darkest before the dawn."

"Most of the work in the world is done by people who don't feel well."

"Never let them see you sweat."

"Your worth is equal to how hard you work."

Perhaps a visit with a family member regarding this question could initiate a great conversation and even a heart-to-heart talk. When you think you have identified one of your family mottos—or something close to it—write it down.

Think about

What influence did your family motto have on you while you were growing up?

Did you accept it as true? Did you resent it?

How does it influence you today?

Write about

What is my family motto?
How has it influenced my life?

Another way to uncover or discover those beliefs that influence you—those core beliefs that influence *all* you think, say, and do—is to complete the following sentences:

A good husband____
A good wife____
A good daughter of an ill father_____________________________
A good employee_______________________________________
A good person who is under stress____________________________

Well, you get the picture. Think of one of your present roles or situations in your life and write about what you think a "good" person in that role and situation is like or does.

Can you see some of your beliefs peeking out, showing their heads, perhaps even their hands?

Let's explore how those beliefs influence your ability to solve your problems.

Solving Our Problems

Think about some problem in your life that you would love to solve and ask yourself if any of your beliefs—about yourself, others, life, or love—are

- Perpetuating the problem?
- Contributing to the problem?
- Preventing solutions?
- *The* problem?

I am going to offer you several examples, but see what comes to your mind at this point. You can always change your answer.

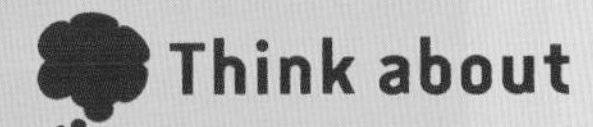

Think about

What beliefs about myself hold me captive?

What beliefs about another person constrain me?

What beliefs about life prevent me from moving forward?

What beliefs about love prevent me
from giving and receiving love?

Write about

Identify one belief that is
connected to your problem.

Write it down.

A Helpful Question

Here is a question that will allow you to challenge that old "hindering, constraining belief" and open up new possibilities. It is the "If I were to believe" question. I have witnessed its positive influence in helping people, over and over again.[3]

It goes like this:

If I were to believe ________________ (insert a helpful belief), what would be different?

Consider the following example:

A woman was held captive by a belief that she was worthless. That belief was planted by some cruel words spoken to her by her father when she was just a young girl. One day she was willing to really think about—and pray about—one question. And that made all the difference.

The question was:

If I were to believe that my father was grieved about the words he misspoke so many years ago and I saw a videotape of him pacing the floor at 2 A.M., weeping and crying out, "I am so sorry for the pain I caused my daughter. I am so sorry that I made her doubt herself," what would be different for me?

How to develop a useful "If I were to believe" question

How can you develop an "If I were to believe" question that can open up new possibilities for you and even change your life?

1. Identify the hindering or constraining belief that presently holds you captive and is perpetuating the problem. Example: God does not love me.
2. Insert a helpful or facilitating belief that would free you and support solutions. Example: I am a child of God who loves me.

It is important to note that the helpful belief may be the complete opposite of the original nonhelpful belief. In fact, it probably will be.

3. Pose the question.

Try it

You've written down your old constraining belief that was causing you problems.

Now think of a helpful, different belief, perhaps even one that is vastly different—**180 degrees** different—from your old constraining belief. What comes to mind?

Anything?

Examples

Let's look at some real-life examples where I offered this type of question. Note the remarkable changes that followed.

A couple was in constant conflict because of the husband's chronic back pain. He was becoming a "chronic pain" to his wife due to his physical complaints and limitations. Their present constraining belief was that there was nothing they could do to influence the husband's physical pain and that things were only going to get worse. I asked them to consider the following questions:

If you were to believe that you had 10 percent more control over the pain than you presently believe you have, what would be different in your marriage?

If you were to believe that you could unite as a couple against the pain, what do you think might happen? How would you do that?

Those questions opened up a conversation between the husband and wife that allowed them to face the problem together. When it became a joint effort to deal with the challenge, the couple were infused with hope and energy. They left our meeting and solved their marital problems on their own. These questions changed the couple's focus and helped propel them forward.

A wife was very discouraged. Her husband's brother had died, and she had offered all kinds of comfort and counsel to her husband in an effort to help. He was in such grief, he didn't know what to do. Based on his actions, she believed that her husband didn't want her help and was upset with her. She was starting to pull away from him. Both were suffering.

I asked the wife the following simple question, which was 180 degrees different from the belief that was influencing her withdrawing behavior and hurt feelings:

If you were to believe that your husband cares deeply about your efforts to help him grieve, what would you do more or less of?

We know that things are not always as they appear—especially to each of us individually. Could it be that her husband really did appreciate her efforts and just didn't have the energy or ability to show it?

As she considered the "If you were to believe" question, she began to see things—especially her husband—differently. She relaxed and began to notice his appreciation for her efforts. One question did all that!

A woman was in deep distress over her husband's addiction to pornography, which she had just discovered. When confronted with the situation, the husband was sincerely repentant and was willing to do everything to free himself and his marriage from this plague.

I asked the wife the following question:

If you were to discover that your husband had been on his knees, praying into the night for freedom from his addiction, how would you join with him in his fight against pornography?

Her heart softened. His resolve increased. Together they won their fight against pornography and their marriage was saved.

Elderly parents sometimes believe that they should not talk about family problems, even when everyone knows the problems are there. In one family with grown children, the problems had been simmering for decades and no one had ever dared talk about them—especially with the parents present. One question invited the elderly parents to resume their positions as patriarch and matriarch of their family, establishing their roles as guardians of their family:

If you were to believe that as the parents of this family it is an important job for you to speak up, what would you speak up about?

With this new perspective, the parents felt as though they finally had permission to speak about what had been troubling them and all family members. A healing conversation—tearful and tender at times—with other family members ensued. Problems were clearly identified without blame. Solutions were generated. Hearts were healed. It was important that this happened at this time for this family because just a few months later the father died.

A repentant man was back in full fellowship with the Church—but not with his wife. She seemed unwilling, unable really, to forgive his sins and move forward with their marriage and family life. Constraining beliefs about repentance and forgiveness held her captive. The following question started to shift things for her:

If you were to read the life history of your husband since his rebaptism and discover that the Lord had left out any reference to the struggles and sins that led to your husband's excommunication, what would begin to change for you?

Write about
Fill in the blank on your own "If I were to believe" question by inserting a helpful, 180-degree-different belief from the present belief that constrains you and perpetuates the problem:
If I were to believe
______________________________,
what would be different?
What would I be able to do that I can't do now?

SOME OTHER HELPFUL QUESTIONS

Let's try some other sentence stems to help you.
Instead of "If you were to believe," try these:

If I were to discover . . .
(insert a belief that is dramatically different from that which you currently believe)

If I were to remember . . .
(again, insert a belief that is very different from that which you presently hold)

Did that help?
Try this one as well to help you open your heart to a new helpful belief:

If for the next ten minutes I were to believe . . .
(insert helpful belief), ***what difference would that make?***

Or this:

I don't really believe this, but if I were to believe . . . (insert helpful belief that is 180-degrees different from your present belief), ***what would be different?***

Write about your answers.
Take your time.

Now let's use the "If I were to believe" question to embed some truths into our hearts and minds, to invite us to live up to our privileges, to be our true selves.

What comes to your mind and to your heart as you prayerfully consider the following statements of eternal truth?

YOU DON'T NEED TO BE ALONE

If you were to believe that the Holy Ghost really could be your constant companion—and if you could picture Him right there beside you—how would you manage this very difficult relationship situation?

There is a chapter later in this book entirely devoted to this question, but see what comes to your mind now.

SOMEONE MAY BE TRYING TO HELP

Think of a troublesome situation you have with another person. It feels as though you are caught in a vicious cycle.

Now ask yourself this question:

If I were to believe that my husband (or wife, friend, sister) really loves me and that his or her behavior—the very behavior that has caused me concern or even annoyed me the most—has actually been his or her very best effort to draw close to me and to help solve our problems, what would change?

MARITAL INTIMACY IS A SACRED GOD-GIVEN EXPRESSION OF LOVE

If you were to believe that marital intimacy can be a kind of sacred God-given expression—a time which can draw you and your spouse closer together and to the Lord—how would you want to prepare differently for that experience?

You are preparing for marital intimacy with the thoughts you have about men and women and love and marriage—every day of your life. If you believe Lucifer's lies about sexual relationships, you will never experience what the Lord intended for a husband and wife to share.

Try it

Now that you've been immersed in several other examples of using the "If I were to believe" question, try again to write one for yourself. Look at one of your relationships and consider how you might see something different in others, and in the way you relate to them, if you were to use the "If I were to believe" question.

Let that kind of question help you escape from some of those old hindering, constraining beliefs that are holding you and your heart and your life captive. Try it. Have fun with it.

Write about

- What you've learned about beliefs.
- One hindering or constraining belief you have recognized.
- One helpful belief you want to embrace, which will set you free!

And now let me offer you two last sets of "If you were to believe" questions that should really be stated as *"If you were to remember the truth"* questions.

Here they are. Let's put these last two questions in first person—for you!

Ask yourself:

If I really were to remember that there is power in the Atonement for me (healing power, enabling power, purifying power, saving power), what difference would that make in my life?

What would I be able to do that I can't do now?

And this last one:

If I really were to remember that there is power in the Atonement for me—

What questions would I stop asking?

What questions would I start asking?

How would my life be different?

CHAPTER 5

SEVEN QUESTIONS THAT CAN CHANGE YOUR LIFE

A friend posed a question one day that triggered the thoughts resulting in this chapter. My friend is a wife, mother, grandmother, psychologist, and stake Relief Society president. She is also thoughtful, prayerful, very smart, and inclined to think far beneath the surface about things. Her question came as a result of pondering how to help the sisters in her stake. Her question was simply:

"What are your favorite and most helpful questions to ask?"

The following seven questions are my answer to her question.

QUESTION #1 WHAT IS ON MY PREMORTAL LIST OF THINGS TO DO WHILE ON EARTH?

What were you born to do?

Why are you here on earth? Especially now?

Why not twenty years from now? Why not in the 1800s?

Why were you born (or adopted) into your particular family?

Why were you born into your race or nationality?

Why were you born at all?

HAVE YOU EVER CONSIDERED THESE QUESTIONS:

What is the wonderful mission for which I was sent to earth?

What do I need to do to fill the measure of my creation?

The Prophet Joseph Smith taught that if a person could gaze into heaven for five minutes, he would know more about heaven than if he studied the topic forever.[1]

Here's a hypothetical idea worth considering. The Lord has wisely drawn a veil over our memories, but just imagine the effect it would have on your life if you were permitted to watch ten minutes of your premortal DVD. Now, whether our premortal lives are recorded on a DVD I'm not sure, but I love to think about the perspective those recordings would bring to our lives.

I believe that if you were to see yourself—your true premortal self—for just ten minutes, and were to observe how you behaved, what you did, commitments you made, people you associated with, who your mentors and teachers were, the strength you demonstrated, who you sustained (meaning Jesus Christ)—I believe *all* of your present confusion, doubts, struggles, and problems would fall away! Now that's a powerful perspective—the power of the perspective of your premortal valiancy and commitments.

I believe if you could see what you said you would do here on earth, you might say, "Oh, now I understand! Even this really difficult situation makes sense to me now."

Each of us came to earth with a scroll attached to our spirits—so to speak—entitled

The gospel teaches us that there were two very important items listed for everyone:

1. Receive a mortal body.

2. Be tested[2] and demonstrate that I will *"do all things whatsoever the Lord [my] God shall command [me]"* (Abraham 3:25).

We know there is a third item on that premortal scroll:

Find and fulfill my mortal mission

President Joseph F. Smith taught the following about our missions on earth:

"He that sent His Only Begotten Son into the world to accomplish the mission which he did, also sent every soul within the sound of my voice, and indeed every man and woman in the world, to accomplish a mission, and that mission cannot be accomplished by neglect; nor by indifference; nor can it be accomplished in ignorance. We must learn our duty; learn the requirements that the Lord has made at our hands, *and understand the responsibilities that he has placed upon us."*[3]

President Smith's statement underlines an important question for each of us:

Why are you here on earth—at this particular time?

For example:

Have you been asked to shepherd strong-willed spirits and help build them into talented, faithful men and women?

Does your life's mission include helping others find and fulfill theirs?

Have you been asked to learn to distinguish good from evil and bravely speak up against practices that support the adversary's agenda?

Or will your life's mission require you to sacrifice in a particular way for the mission of another?

Have you been sent to live in a troubled family situation in order to increase the purity in that lineage by putting a stop—once and for all—to various impure practices?

Have you been assigned to teach with clarity the eternal truths that will help the women and men of the world and their families?

Will you bring charity—truly the pure love of Christ—to a situation from which most people would draw back?

What is the part *you* are to play in helping the Savior with His mission, which is to bring to pass the immortality and eternal life of man?

Just as Esther was, we were indeed born *"for such a time as this"* (Esther 4:14).

And the truth about finding our mission is this:

Because we love the Lord and have faith in Him, we want to be obedient to Him and be an instrument in His hands.

We want to do whatever He asks us to do.

We are willing and happy to be, as Paul described himself, *"a prisoner of Jesus Christ"* (Philemon 1:1).

It is our obedience to the Lord that positions us to fill the measure of our creation.

The more obedient we are to Him, the more we grow into our true selves and the more we are able to do what we came here to do.

Increasingly impeccable obedience is key to finding your mission.

And consecration is key to fulfilling your mission once you've found it!

The only way I know to do what we've come here to do—to live up to who we are and to worthily fulfill our premortal commitments, our life's mission—is to consecrate all that we have and all that we are to the Lord.

That means putting Him and His work first.

That means using our gifts and talents to build up His kingdom rather than our own.

That means surrendering everything to Him, even our will.

If we are to make sense of mortality, it is essential to understand that we had a premortal existence as spirit children of Heavenly Parents. We lived eons of years with Them. We were tutored by Them. We loved Them and were loved by Them.

Without that perspective, it is difficult to make sense of the times in our lives when we suffer or struggle, when we can't seem to improve our situation, or when we lose a loved one—times when things seem anything but fair. In such times, it helps to remember where we came from, what is expected of us in mortality, and where we are headed.

Lacking that eternal vision of who and whose we truly are, those who are without a knowledge of the gospel try to find meaning in the philosophies of men. And history shows the futility of that!

In fact, if we omit the reality that we lived premortally as spirit children of our Heavenly Parents and have been born into mortality to demonstrate our ability to be obedient in a quest to return to Them, and to find and fulfill our life's mission, how can anyone make sense of this life?

Your Mission

Should you choose to accept it . . .

The truth is

- We had premortal identity and experiences.
- We developed premortal associations.
- Premortally, we were given missions to fulfill while on earth.

Caution: Before we go any farther, it is important to draw a distinction between premortally being given a mission to fulfill on earth—and predestination. There is a huge difference and that difference is the eternal law of agency. While the heresy of predestination negates agency by teaching that people's lives are basically pre-programmed, the truths surrounding our life's missions *require* agency.

We have opportunities to find and fulfill our missions, but we don't have to. No one is making us do it. We have our agency to choose how we will spend our time and energy and talents and resources while we are here on earth. All of that, in fact, is part of our testing.

The outcome is in *our own* hands: Will we choose to find and fulfill our missions or not? It's our choice. It's up to each one of us.

A TRANSITION CERTIFICATE

Imagine how helpful a "transition certificate" would be to help us segue from our premortal realm to life on earth. The certificate might be delivered with the newborn child and say something such as:

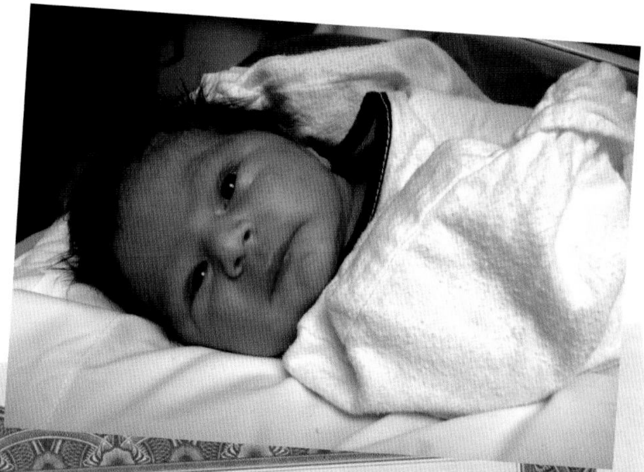

This is ______________ (insert your own name).

She was a loyal supporter of the Savior.

Because she won't be able to remember her prior existence, please teach her the plan of salvation and to have faith in the Atonement of Jesus Christ. She has already overcome __________ and __________ and __________.

She has made the following commitments to her Heavenly Parents:

__________ __________ __________

Please support her in keeping these commitments.

Your role as parents is to help her

- Remember and recognize the voice of the Lord and the promptings of the Holy Ghost.
- Remember and embrace the truths of the gospel of Jesus Christ and gain a testimony of the Restoration.
- Remember and understand why she came to earth.
- Remember and seek to fulfill the mortal opportunities she foresaw which made her shout for joy (Job 38:7).

As you read the scriptures with her, she will recognize the Spirit that is in them and the feeling of being immersed in truth.

As you love her, she will remember the love she experienced with her Heavenly Parents and the Lord Jesus Christ. This may make her feel lonely sometimes because of the stark difference between the finest love offered on earth and the intensely profound experience of the pure love of God.

As you teach her the truths of the restored gospel of Jesus Christ, she will begin to develop her own testimony of the plan of salvation and of her premortal existence—of who she really is, and what is expected of her here on earth to help to build up the kingdom of God.

Have you found your TRUE PURPOSE ?

Can you imagine the public's reaction if a popular talk show host suddenly declared that he or she had discovered that there was a premortal existence? That we had received certain missions there that we were to complete here on earth? And that one of the major purposes of life is to identify and fulfill those missions?

How excited would the people of the world be? How quickly would a major marketing blitz be launched, encouraging women and men to find their true purposes in life? Can you imagine the campaign to urge people not to spend one more minute on anything that wasn't going to move them toward finding their missions?

Can you imagine the television shows that might spring up, detailing individual efforts and successes? Can you imagine the flurry of activity many would make to ensure they could watch the final episode of such a gripping reality series?

What would the slogans on T-shirts, mugs, posters, bumper stickers, and Internet pop-up ads say in order to encourage people to stop whatever they were doing—however important or urgent they thought it was—and go steadily forward with faith to find their missions, even their commissions from our Father in Heaven?

What would the world do if it believed what we know to be true?

But the world hasn't embraced these truths—and never will!

That is what makes our quest to live as covenant women and men of God all the more complicated and adventurous! Because if we are following the Lord, we will feel increasingly out of sync with the world. In fact, perhaps an early clue that there is something not quite right in our lives is if we are feeling a little *too* comfortable with the world and looking and acting a little too much like the women and men of the world.

WHAT IS ON MY PREMORTAL DVD?

WHAT IS ON MY PREMORTAL "THINGS TO DO WHILE ON EARTH" LIST?

What difference would it make if we were to live with a constant awareness of the reality of our premortal existence and a daily quest to fulfill our mortal missions?

The possibility that there is a such a list and a premortal DVD is both marvelous and sobering news. Let's start with the marvelous news. Consider these two recent real-life examples:

1. A woman, whose daughter had joined the Church ten years earlier, but who had herself been hesitant to hear the truths of the restored gospel of Jesus Christ, attended a gathering of predominantly LDS women with her daughter. The mother heard the concepts of a premortal DVD and of the possibility of a "Things to Do While on Earth" list taught at the gathering. Those ideas struck her like a thunderbolt to her heart.

Right in the meeting and at the very moment these truths were spoken, she turned to her daughter and said out loud, "Well, what do I do now?" Her daughter didn't know what her mother was talking about.

The mother explained the spiritual experience she had, and she was baptized soon after that event.

This wonderful woman, whose spirit leaped at hearing those truths, is growing into the magnificent woman of God that she really is. And every day she is mindful of, even vigilant about, discovering the items on her "Things to Do While on Earth" list.

2. In the midst of a really difficult situation—physically, spiritually, emotionally, and mentally—one woman found great comfort and courage as she thought and prayed about the following question:

To what did I agree in the premortal world that my Heavenly Father is honoring and is therefore not able to respond to my present request?[4]

What mission were you given to accomplish while you are here on earth?

Because that information is lost to us at birth, the only way we can discover what our mortal missions are is to pray and ask the Lord to reveal them to us. It is my testimony that amazing things can happen when we let our Heavenly Father know that we are serious, when we pray:

"Please help me to fill the measure of my creation; please help me to fulfill the wonderful mission for which I was sent to earth."

And when we are in the midst of surviving something unbelievably difficult—even hideous—when the Spirit whispers the assurance that this is part of our life mission and is on our "to do" list, everything changes. Our perspective enlarges as our vision clears. Our energy flows. Our faith in the Lord and our courage and ability to endure increase.

Now the sobering news:

If you are not finding and fulfilling your mortal mission, it really doesn't matter what else you are doing.

You will not be happy. That's a guarantee. Even though the world, and perhaps even those you love, may be cheering you on in your life's work and successes, your spirit will be churning as time goes on. You'll think there is something wrong with you, but actually, there will be something really right. Your spirit, under the influence of the Spirit, will be trying to get your attention to inform you that you are spending your time doing all kinds of things that are *not* part of your mission and that you don't really have time to do.

What is your mission and whom did you say you would reconnect with to assist in building up the kingdom of God here on earth?

If you are spending all kinds of time with people who are working against your mission and your premortal commitments, you're not going to be happy. If you are not in the right places to reconnect with those you said you'd help or join forces with here, loneliness will be your companion all the days of your life.

Ponder this thought by the apostle Orson F. Whitney:

"Why are we drawn toward certain persons, and they toward us, independently of any known previous acquaintance? Is it a fact, or only a fancy, that we and they were mutually acquainted and mutually attracted in some earlier period of our eternal existence? Is there something, after all, in that much abused term 'affinity,' and is this the basis of its claim? More than once, after meeting someone whom I had never met before on earth, I have wondered why his or her face seemed so familiar. Many times, upon hearing a noble sentiment expressed, though unable to recall having heard it until then, I have been thrilled by it, and felt as if I had always known it. The same is true of music, some strains of which are like echoes from afar, sounds falling from celestial heights, notes struck from the vibrant harps of eternity. I do not assert pre-acquaintance in all such cases, but as one thought suggests another, these queries arise in the mind."[5]

Could the joy expressed in this picture of two of my great-nieces represent the joy our spirits feel when we are reunited with those we associated with premortally?

Think about

Imagine what you might see if the veil were lifted and you were permitted to view your premortal DVD for just ten minutes.

What do you already suspect is part of your mortal mission and is on your "Things to Do While on Earth" list?

Do you wish you could see your personal premortal list of "Things to Do While on Earth"? What does your mission involve?

Have you had the experience of doing something heart-wrenchingly difficult and thinking, "Oh, yes, that was probably on my 'to-do' list"?

Have you been able to sense at least one time in your life that you were doing something of eternal importance to you, despite the rigor of the task?

What do you suppose the Lord wants you to learn through your efforts to find and to fulfill your life's mission? Faith? Charity? Patience?

And speaking of patience, do *you* feel a growing urgency, an impatience, to do all that the Lord requires of you so that you can fulfill your life's mission?

You can be certain you were commissioned to do something—and probably many "somethings"—for the Lord. And finding your life's mission is crucial to finding happiness in this life.

I think of a great woman—a wife, mother, and grandmother—who has recently been focused on gaining a better understanding of her life's mission. After Christmas she called me, concerned and seeking, and related the following:

"For our Christmas I did all the right things. We had wonderful food and scripture readings. The children performed the nativity. We sang carols and took photographs. We celebrated the Savior's birth as a family and had a marvelous time being together.

"But now that Christmas is over, I'm looking for more meaning in my life."

Perhaps the intense focus on the Savior stirred her spirit to want to serve Him even more.

What a spiritually in-tune woman! His Spirit is moving upon her spirit, letting her know that there is yet more to her mission on earth. She wants to do all that she was born to do.

She wants to do all those things that are part of her mortal mission.

Even though she is doing all kinds of "right things," her spirit can tell there is something more—or something different—she needs to be doing. As she thought about it, she realized that missionary work has always stirred her soul. Could it be that she—and her gifts for searching out missionary moments and preaching the gospel with simplicity and power—was brought to the kingdom for such a time as this?

I hope you are in a mindset similar to my friend and are looking for more meaning in your life.

If you feel a little unsettled these days, the reason may be that you are not yet fulfilling the wonderful mission for which you were sent to earth.

Does that mean that you need to make a dramatic change?

It may—

But—it may not.

Just the other day I had an unexpected conversation with a friend who has felt very restless and underused. She is a faithful, multitalented, capable woman, and yet she said, almost in despair, *"I wonder if I even have a mission!"*

Later, she poured her heart out to the Lord, just as she has been doing relentlessly for months. However, this time she listened in a different way and received a little "corrective feedback" from the Lord. She had been looking for her mission somewhere other than in the situation in which He has presently placed her.

Through the whisperings of the Spirit, her mind was enlarged and her heart changed.

Her mind was flooded with ideas—ideas confirming that she was in exactly the right place for what the Lord needs her to do.

No one was more surprised than she.

What difference would it make in our lives if we were to look at every ability and every talent, every challenge and grueling obstacle, as having a premortal origin?

I believe that every gift and endowment from above, and every opportunity, every heartache and disappointment here, teaches us, enlightens us, and makes us who we are: women and men better prepared to serve the Lord, however and whenever He calls.

And what happens to our souls when the only desire of our hearts is to give back all that we have and are to the Lord?

When we willingly consecrate every gift, talent, and resource?

When we want to consecrate every relationship unto Him?

What happens?

Marvelous things!

Life-changing and spirit-enlarging things!

For example, do you have a musical talent? What happens to your practice and your performances as you consecrate that talent to the Lord?

Or do you have an artistic ability to create something wonderful out of almost nothing?

Or a talent to teach with clarity?

Or to bring family history to life with stories, pictures, and music?

Or to make people feel welcomed and included?

Or to demonstrate compassion for others?

Or to act as a peacemaker?

Chances are you developed those abilities in your premortal existence, so it's no wonder that your spirit yearns to use them now to help build up the kingdom of God here on the earth.

That's what you were born to do.

Think about

What comes to your mind and heart when you really think about consecrating your abilities to the Lord to help build up His kingdom? What do you want to do more of? Less of?

If you were to consecrate a relationship unto the Lord, what do you think might happen to your ability to give and to receive love, to be patient, to put contention aside, to give others the benefit of the doubt?

When you think about truly devoting your life for the good of building up the Lord's kingdom, what changes for you?

Now, if you've been tempted to second-guess the Lord with thoughts such as, "Well, the Lord would never use me to do anything significant for His kingdom," or, "I don't have what it takes to move His work ahead," please consider the following truth as taught by Elder Russell M. Nelson:

"The Lord uses the unlikely to accomplish the impossible."[6]

If you feel like the most unlikely person to be asked to accomplish something that looks utterly impossible, look out!

Consider the Prophet Joseph Smith, who described himself as *"an obscure boy . . . of no consequence"* (JS–H 1:22), yet was the vessel the Lord used in restoring the gospel of Jesus Christ to earth; or Elisabeth, who was far beyond childbearing age, yet gave birth to John, the forerunner of the Savior (Luke 1:5–25, 57–80).

The Lord knows you.

He loves you.

He believes in you.

And He is counting on you to do exactly what you said you would do, to fulfill the wonderful mission for which you were sent to earth.

Happily, you don't have to do it alone.

He stands waiting for us to seek His help.

He is eager to endow those who qualify with His power.

He will gift us with skill and understanding commensurate with our desire, our purity, and our need.

We are part of a royal army of women and men sent here to gather the good women and men of the earth and welcome them into the Lord's kingdom. Indeed, *"we have a labor to perform whilst in this tabernacle of clay, that we may conquer the enemy of all righteousness"* (Moroni 9:6).

In conclusion, affirming that we each have a life mission, which we were sent here to earth to fulfill, allow me to paraphrase the ninth Article of Faith:

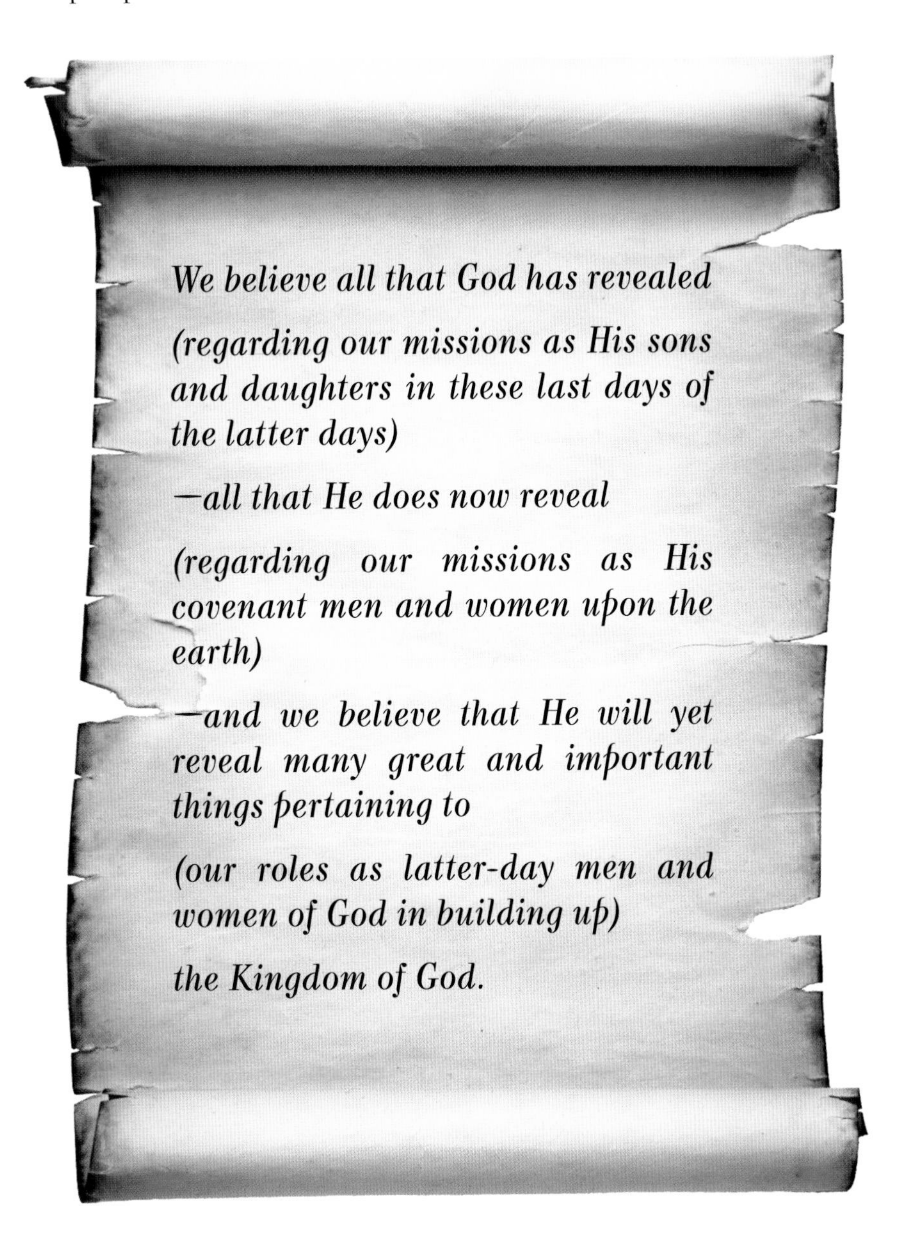

If you are really serious about being happy and at peace,
think about and pray to know:

WHAT IS THE WONDERFUL MISSION FOR WHICH I WAS SENT TO EARTH?

WHAT DO I NEED TO DO TO FILL THE MEASURE OF MY CREATION?

WHAT IS ON MY PREMORTAL LIST OF "THINGS TO DO WHILE ON EARTH"?

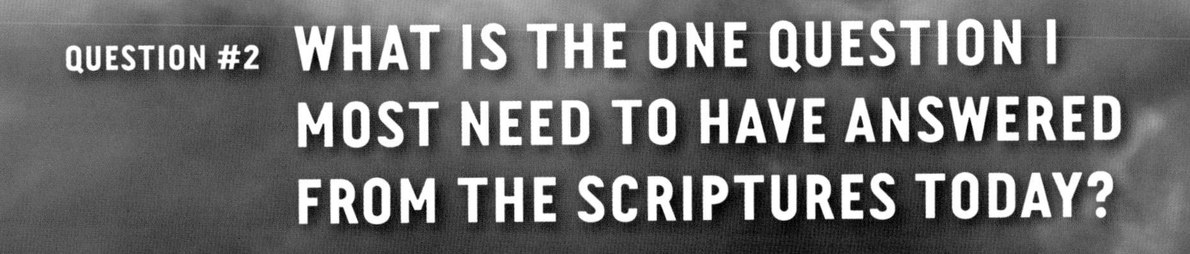

QUESTION #2

WHAT IS THE ONE QUESTION I MOST NEED TO HAVE ANSWERED FROM THE SCRIPTURES TODAY?

"Feast upon the words of Christ; for behold, the words of Christ will tell you all things what ye should do" (2 Nephi 32:3; *emphasis added*).

Do you notice that there is no asterisk after the word *all* indicating exceptions to that promise? There is no asterisk because there are *no* exceptions!

The promise is real:

FEAST UPON THE WORDS OF CHRIST, AND THEY WILL SHOW YOU WHAT YOU SHOULD DO IN *EVERY* SITUATION.

Do you believe that the teachings of Christ will give you answers to *all* of your questions? Very personal answers to very personal questions? Could that really be so?

Let me share a well-kept secret (for many) about the scriptures:

Every question in your life can be answered through the word of the Lord.

The scriptures are answer books!

What a fabulous truth! The words of Christ—as brought to us through the scriptures and the words of His apostles and prophets—will tell us everything we should do.

How to handle every situation in life? *Yes!*

How to deal with everything from financial to family problems? *Yes!*

Does that sound too good to be true? Well, it's not. It's true. The only people who don't believe it are those who haven't tried it.

Would you like to try?

Are you interested?

Would you like to try an experiment that can turn your scriptures into your very own personal answer books?

Think about

What is the most pressing problem in your life today?

What question hangs heavy on your heart and mind—and perhaps has for a long time?

Would you like the answer to your question? Today?

Would you like to know how to proceed? Today?

Before we explore this concept further, let's think about what our options are.

1. We can look to the world.
2. We can look to the word of the Lord.

Isaiah pointed out how displeased the Lord is when we look to the world and not to Him for our counsel:

"Woe to the rebellious children, saith the Lord, that take counsel, but not of me; and that cover with a covering, but not of my spirit, that they may add sin to sin" (Isaiah 30:1).

After tempests and earthquakes and fires and whirlwinds, a pleading voice is heard. It is the Lord saying, "How oft would I have gathered you as a hen gathereth her chickens under her wings." He pleads with and tells the people how often He has yearned to help them; to comfort them; to nurture, take care of, and protect them. And then come four words that always haunt me:

"And ye would not!" (3 Nephi 10:5).

These four words are filled with disappointment and heartache.

Consider what the Lord has given us. Consider all that He *wants* to give us. How many times do we turn away from the very help that would heal, lift, free, and strengthen us? Do you think we sometimes make Him sad? In what ways have you and I been resisting the love of the Lord, the help of the Savior? How many times have we looked to the world instead of to Him for help? Would He say to us today:

"How often would I have gathered you, (fill in your name), healed you, freed you, helped you, delivered you, comforted you . . . **and ye would not!** You looked elsewhere when I was right here and willing to help you."

How often might the Lord say to us:

- I gave you the fulness of my gospel, and you accepted only part of my truths and ordinances, and you were embarrassed and annoyed by the rest.
- I gave you priesthood power to act in my name, and you did not learn how to draw upon that power or live worthily to use it (D&C 121:36–37).
- I gave you the law of tithing to solve all your financial problems, but you would not live it!
- I gave you my words as recorded in the scriptures and as brought to you by living prophets and apostles, and you would not study them. You wouldn't let them guide you on a daily basis. You would not search the scriptures for the answers to your problems (2 Nephi 32:7).
- I gave you the Word of Wisdom to increase your health and keep you safe from the cunning deceptions of marketers, and you would not live it fully (D&C 89:4).
- I gave you the Holy Ghost to be with you when I could not—to guide, direct, and protect you and to assuage your loneliness—and you would not receive Him.
- I gave you sacred temple ordinances, which would have bound you and your family together eternally—so that being together forever would not just be a lovely thought, but could be a reality—and you ignored my invitation.
- I gave you the Atonement so you wouldn't have to feel guilty and ravaged by your sins all the days of your life, nor would you have to live a life tainted with sin, and you refused to accept my cleansing, healing, enabling, enlivening power.
- I offered you eternal life—the kind of life I live—***and you would not!***

No. You would not look to me. You looked *instead* to the world to solve your problems.

We embrace truth wherever we may find it,[1] but often our problem in seeking help is that what is offered as truth is not really true. It's just the *best idea* that someone can give to us at *the present time*.

What can we count on when we seek answers to our problems from the world? The answers may change depending upon whom you talk to and depending upon how new the theory is upon which the answer is based. We can always count on change when it comes to the theories, suggestions, and instructions of the world, because they always do!

In stark contrast, as the Spirit of the Lord teaches us the word of the Lord, He will bring to our hearts and minds the wisdom we are lacking.

When we seek answers to our problems from the word of the Lord, we can trust that the wisdom is real and true and long-lasting, even eternal—wisdom that you can count on, very personal wisdom for your very personal questions.

So now let me offer you an experiment that will unlock the scriptures for you and turn them into your personal answers-for-life books.

The *Take a Daily Question to the Scriptures for 30 Days* Experiment

Begin each of the thirty days of this experiment by asking yourself:

What is the one question I most need to have answered today[2]—
the question that is burning in my heart and mind, burdening me—
the question that is troubling my life?

Then:

- Take your scriptures and kneel down and thank your Heavenly Father, in the name of Jesus Christ, for the scriptures.
- Ask for the Spirit to be with you as you seek an answer to your one question for that day. Picture the Holy Ghost being right there with you as you read.
- Ask your Heavenly Father the one question you most need to have answered that day.
- Open your scriptures and read until you find the answer.

It is my experience, and the witness of so many others, that you won't have to read very far before you will find what you are looking for.

Record Your Experiences

Take a piece of paper and make four columns. Label the four columns:

- Date
- Question Asked
- Scriptural Reference of Answer
- Answer

The reason you'll want to record the scriptural reference is that often the same scripture will take on a new meaning for you the next time you go to that reference. Have you noticed that before? That is how personal revelation works. It's personal. Very personal. And it's just for you, at that very moment.

You may ask: *Well, do I ask the same question every day for thirty days?*

Ask the question that you most need to have answered for that particular day. Maybe it *is* the same question as the day before, or a few days ago. Maybe it is an entirely different question each day for thirty days. Thirty different questions could be asked in thirty days. Or twenty or fifteen or one. You will know. In the very process of determining *which* question to take to the scriptures that day, you will be guided, and perhaps taught.

You may wonder: *How can that process work? Why does it work?*

1. It works because the Lord has promised us:

> *"Ask, and it shall be given you; seek, and ye shall find; knock, and it shall be opened unto you: For every one that asketh receiveth; and he that seeketh findeth; and to him that knocketh it shall be opened"* (Matthew 7:7–8).

That's exactly what this thirty-day experiment is all about.

- You are *asking* the Lord for an answer from His words.
- You are *seeking*. You are searching the scriptures, with the assistance of the Holy Ghost to enlighten your mind and open the eyes of your understanding.
- You are *finding* answers to questions—your life questions which have burdened your mind and heart.
- And you are showing your gratitude to the Lord for those answers and for the entire revelatory process by recording it for your future review and instruction.

2. It works because the Holy Ghost is helping you to receive personal revelation through the words of Christ.

When we let the Lord know that we are serious about finding answers to our life problems, challenges, concerns, and crises through *His* word, He gives us everything we ask and more. In just a thirty-day period we can begin to experience the truth expressed in Doctrine and Covenants 121:33.

"As well might man stretch forth his puny arm to stop the Missouri river in its decreed course, or to turn it up stream, as to hinder the Almighty from pouring down knowledge from heaven upon the heads of the Latter-day Saints."

Sometimes the knowledge and wisdom you receive as you take a question to the scriptures may feel like a manna's portion—just enough to get you through that one day. And at other times, the pouring forth of knowledge will be like a steady stream, filling every cup that you have to overflowing.

WHAT CAN HAPPEN AS YOU FOLLOW A COURSE OF SEARCHING THE SCRIPTURES FOR ANSWERS TO YOUR LIFE DILEMMAS?

- *Your confidence will begin to grow because you will know where to find answers to your problems.*
- *You will be far less stressed when yet another problem arises because you will know where to go for guidance and direction.*
- *You will begin to grow in your ability to feast on the words of Christ.*
- *You will truly experience His words showing you all things that you should do.*
- *You will feel your faith growing—your faith in the Savior and His words.*
- *You will feel an increased ability to hear the voice of the Lord through the Spirit and through His words, the scriptures.*
- *And you will "stand all amazed" at the love and the light the Savior offers you through His words.*

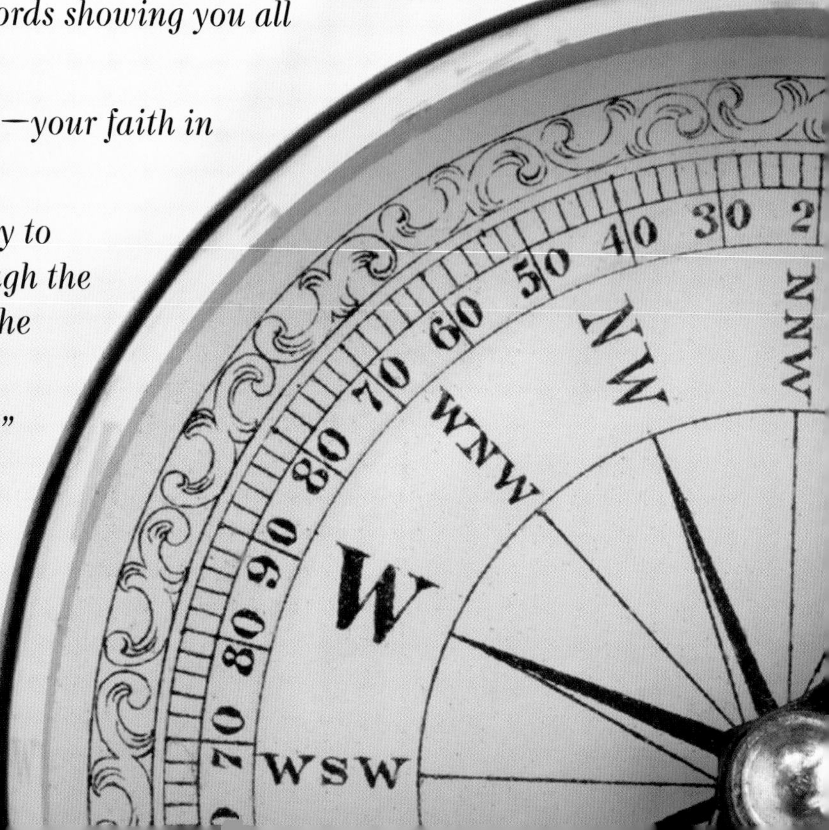

Q What can happen when you take your questions to the scriptures?

A You can have truths brought to your mind beyond what is written on the page of scripture.

A counselor in a stake presidency shared his experience:

"I just wanted to share with you the experience I had this morning, taking your challenge to take a question to the scriptures daily for thirty days, and receive answers to our questions, through the reading of our scriptures.

"Let me start by telling you that last night I was looking up information on lds.org for some thoughts from the Brethren to include in the talk that I am preparing for the Saturday evening session of our upcoming stake conference. My theme was to be 'Come unto Christ,' and I wanted to share the words of the Savior from 3 Nephi 11 and focus on three principles. But I was feeling last night that I should find something to add to that. I wrestled, trying to find something more.

"Then this morning when I arose to read my scriptures, I thought about your challenge.

"As I opened my scriptures, I found myself being led to 3 Nephi 11. As I was reading, an impression came into my mind very distinctly: 'The scriptures are sufficient for this assignment.'

"I didn't need to look up additional information. I just needed to teach what the Savior said and teach the principles that I have discovered within these verses. At that moment I felt at peace with this impression.

"I had a wonderful spiritual experience. It made for a wonderful day, the rest of the day!"

A woman wrote of her experience:

"Early in the day I had taken one question that was troubling me to the scriptures and, as anticipated, I received an answer that got me through the day. Then just before I went to sleep, I felt drawn to ask one more question. I opened my scriptures and my eyes fell on one verse. But what came to my mind, in addition to the words in the verse, was an entire concept I had never considered before. I ran to my computer and

recorded the thoughts that kept coming to my mind. Because they were so useful and so new to me, I wanted to remember these ideas. I typed as quickly as I could. Four pages later, I was done. By reading just that one verse, the eyes of my understanding were indeed opened. I couldn't believe what had happened. And I am grateful."

Q What can happen when you take your questions to the scriptures?

A You may stand amazed—or maybe a little chagrined—as you recognize the treasures for your life that have been available to you all this time. You may even feel a little grieved that you have been just one question away from all that gold. All you needed to do was ask!

One faithful and devoted Latter-day Saint woman, who has held every possible ward and stake calling, responded to this experiment and discovered the gold mine of the scriptures. She said:

"I've read my scriptures all my life. But no one ever suggested to me that I could find actual answers for my life through the scriptures. This is all brand new for me, and I am loving the adventure! I can't believe this was here all the time. Why didn't anyone teach me this before?"

Q What can happen when you take your questions to the scriptures?

A Your perspective, your life, and your feelings can change!

One young wife and mother wrote the following:

"My best friend and I both started the 30-day challenge to ask questions and have them answered during our study of the scriptures. I cannot express how grateful both of us have

been for this inspired challenge. We have both been amazed at our answers and how this has changed our lives and perspectives. We call one another often (we live in different states) and are amazed at how often we end up asking the same question and receiving the same answers—from different scriptures! . . .

"I find that I have been so much happier as I have taken this opportunity."

Q What can happen when you take your questions to the scriptures?

A You can have the experience recorded by Joseph Smith (Joseph Smith–History) and Joseph F. Smith (D&C 138).

Listen to the words of the Prophet Joseph Smith as he records his experience of reading James 1:5: *"Never did any passage of scripture come with more power to the heart of man than this did at this time to mine. It seemed to enter with great force into every feeling of my heart. I reflected on it again and again"* (JS–H 1:12).

Listen to Joseph F. Smith's words as he writes about his experience reading 1 Peter 3–4: *"As I read I was greatly impressed, more than I had ever been before"* (D&C 138:6).

The scriptures will speak to you in an entirely new way and the eyes of your understanding will be opened (D&C 138:11).

Did you know that the Book of Mormon can help you get a job?

That was one woman's experience. She was newly divorced. Her husband had betrayed their marriage covenant, and she was desperately seeking employment to support her sons. At a time in her life when she, on her own, could barely get herself out of bed because of the emotional upheaval in her heart and mind, she commenced a daily practice of taking whatever question she needed help with—for that particular day—to the scriptures. She fully expected an answer, and she was never disappointed. Day after day, the Spirit opened her eyes to see things that seemed to be written just for her, and for that exact day. Answers to her questions leaped off the pages.

Questions such as:

- *What should I do today?* In the very early days of the divorce, she barely knew where to start. The Book of Mormon helped her prioritize and know what to include and not to include on her daily "to do" list.

- *How can I get a job?* By reading a Book of Mormon passage, she knew exactly how to present herself for a crucial and highly desirable job interview in her field of engineering—and she got the job.

- *How can I solve this problem at work?* After securing the position, she faced some very difficult, work-related problems. Once again, she took her dilemmas to the Book of Mormon and was enlightened to see the solutions, day after day.

- *How should I talk with my ex-husband today so he doesn't get upset and take it out on the boys?* By reading the Book of Mormon, she knew exactly what to say and what not to say to her ex-husband.

- *How can we work together to be good parents for our sons?* Again, the Book of Mormon gave her marvelous truths about how to positively engage her ex-husband in solving typical concerns and problems surrounding their sons, allowing them to work together as parents and not have their sons get caught in the middle.

The miracle of finding solutions to real-life problems in the scriptures is real and can be part of your life.

Here is an e-mail from a bright, talented, faithful young wife and mother:

"I couldn't imagine that a financial problem that has plagued our family for years could be answered through the scriptures. But I thought I would give the experiment a try.

"I opened to the Book of Mormon and began reading, and that reading took me to a footnote that took me to the Doctrine and Covenants. And there I found my answer!

"I shouldn't be, but I am overwhelmed by the power the word of the Lord has to help me and my family in such a personal way. We know what to do now about our huge money problem, and I am so grateful to Him."

Now, a caution:

DO NOT TRY THIS EXPERIMENT AT HOME UNLESS YOU ARE READY TO HAVE YOUR WORLD TURNED UPSIDE DOWN.

One woman diligently tried the experiment for thirty days. At the end of the thirty days she knew their family was to move to a different city. This was something the family had never even considered before, but it was a decision that has blessed them in innumerable ways. Opening the scriptures day after day opened a brand-new and very unexpected life for them.

What can happen in just thirty days?

My testimony is that as you take this challenge and act on it, your experience with the scriptures will change and many other things in your life will also change.

One possible outcome of your thirty-day experiment may be that those you love will see you loving the scriptures and will want to be just like you!

Let me give you an example:

One day I was talking with my little, nearly-four-year-old great-niece, Beth. She told me she had recently learned to play the piano, to sing, and to dance. She was eager for me to take pictures of her doing all of those things. But she was most excited to show me how she could read her scriptures. She then proceeded to pick up her own personal paperback edition of the Book of Mormon, head to the kitchen table—pencil in her right hand to note the verses she particularly liked—and start "to read." Now this little bundle of light and love—and wisdom—cannot really read, but after listening to her parents and older sisters read the scriptures at mealtimes day after day throughout her young life, the following is what was written on her heart. These are Beth's precise words as she "read" her scriptures.

And He spoke unto me, and He talked to me

And His apostles returned and He died

And He listened to me and He loved me

And He was the Truth of God

And He gave me everything I needed

And He was done!

(By Beth Butler, age 3 years and 10 months)

"Let your children memorize the sound of their parents' voices as you read the scriptures to them."

—Elder Russell M. Nelson[5]

Post-test for the Thirty-day Challenge

After taking the thirty-day challenge, see how many of the following have happened for you:

____ I feel an increased ability to resist old temptations.
____ I pray differently.
____ I feel more like my true self.
____ I am more able to distinguish truth from error.
____ I am more able to detect efforts of the adversary to distract me from my life course.
____ I feel a greater desire to walk away from the world.
____ I feel a greater desire to come closer to the Lord than I ever have before.
____ I feel safer than I ever have in my life. The scriptures are my iron rod.
____ I don't worry about things the way I used to.
____ I feel smarter.
____ I experience sacrament meeting differently.
____ I sing the hymns with more meaning and sincerity.
____ I can remember some things better.
____ I can forget the things that are in the past and that should be forgotten.
____ I feel more able to change in a positive way.
____ I feel the guidance and presence of the Holy Ghost in my life in a new and wonderful way.
____ I see things in my patriarchal blessing that I hadn't seen before.
____ I am a kinder and more gentle person.
____ I am more forgiving of others.
____ I have an increased desire to serve and worship in the temple.
____ I feel a greater desire to be a seeker than ever before in my life. I want to keep seeking after all that the Lord will teach me.
____ I want to live to understand more about His restored gospel and all the blessings available through His ordinances.

WHAT IS THE ONE QUESTION YOU MOST NEED TO HAVE ANSWERED FROM THE SCRIPTURES TODAY?

QUESTION #3
WHAT ARE THREE WORDS TO FOLLOW FOR A GREAT LIFE?

Three words on a big sloping roof of an old barn made it all worthwhile: The two extra hours of rigorous driving along a road that was supposed to be a shortcut. Feeling unsafe during long stretches of the country road where there was no cell phone coverage and not one sign of civilization. Another stretch where the only establishment to be seen was a bar—and a couple of men at the side of the road who looked like they were regular customers. Side-swiping rain came out of nowhere just when I was driving through a treacherous area of gigantic earth-moving machines and potholes large enough to consume a small SUV. Construction workers I could barely see motioned me to follow one of their vehicles to safety.

But somewhere along that "shortcut" and before the summer thunderstorm ripped through the skies releasing a deluge of water, I saw three words on that old barn roof. And that made it all worthwhile. Those words riveted my mind.

Now those were words to live by!

What do you think those words were?

Think about it as I tell you a little bit more about how I happened to see those three words—words that can make us happier, stronger, more resilient, more free, and get us back on the right track if we've gotten distracted.

It was the July first weekend in Canada. Now, when you are born and raised in Raymond, Alberta, Canada, there really is only one place you want to be on July 1 and that is at the Raymond parade! You have to be a Raymondite to fully appreciate the thrill that surges through you when you stand on Main Street with all the other Raymondites, or sit in a folding lawn chair, or on the hood of your car, to watch the ward and stake parade floats, the well-groomed horses, high school marching bands, and motorcycles, bikes, and tricycles—all decorated to the hilt—go by.

This July first was especially significant because I had also attended my high school reunion. When the banners from the bands were put away and the candies, which had been thrown to the children from honored guest vehicles and family-reunion flatbed floats, had been consumed, a friend suggested I take a particular road through Montana to make my trip back to Utah a little shorter. It would save me an hour or more—so I was told. I was eager to return home to my husband, who had encouraged me to attend my reunion—and who, with a grin, assured me that he had another assignment that weekend. So a shortcut, even though it was a road I didn't know, sounded like a great plan. And that's how I ended up on the road that led me right by the barn with the three words written on its roof!

THREE WORDS TO FOLLOW FOR A GREAT LIFE!

The three words made me think about my one and only nephew, Brad. When you have only one nephew, you are highly invested in doing everything you can to help him have a great life. You can't make someone have a great life, of course, but you can invite and entice. You can mentor and tutor and . . . well, you'll see.

When Brad was about six years old, I realized how quickly he was growing up and how soon he would be facing some of the difficulties of life. I wondered what I could do, as his aunt, to increase the likelihood that he would make good choices and thereby escape the pain that comes from breaking the Lord's commandments.

Almost immediately I thought about the Word of Wisdom. So, on a visit to Brad and his family, I took Brad aside and asked him what he knew about the Lord's "law of health." I quizzed him, and even at six years of age he could give me all the answers faster than I could think of the next question.

Then I said, "Brad, I want to make an agreement with you. If you will keep the Word of Wisdom exactly as we have talked about it today, when you are eighteen, I will give you one hundred dollars!"

Well, I thought his eyes would pop right out of their sockets. One hundred dollars! To a little six-year-old—especially this little six-year-old boy, who was quite intrigued with money—one hundred dollars is a lot of money. Brad was enlisted! He was determined to live the Word of Wisdom—with exactness. He was going for the gold! Well, the silver dollars!

Each year after that, Brad and I would have our Word of Wisdom interview.

When he was eight: "Brad, did you smoke any cigarettes this year?"

"No, Aunt Wendy."

When he was ten: "Brad, did you drink any coffee or tea this year?"

"No, Aunt Wendy."

When he was twelve: "Brad, did you take any drugs this year?"

"No, Aunt Wendy."

When he was sixteen: "Okay, Brad, now that you are sixteen you are going to start going to parties and dating girls. If you take one sip of an alcoholic drink, that's going to be a pretty expensive sip. It will cost you one hundred dollars! But you choose. Just know that you could blow this entire agreement with only one sip of beer, wine, or anything that contains alcohol!"

"Oh, Aunt Wendy, I'm not going to do that!"

And the great news was that he didn't!

So, when he was eighteen, following our annual interview, I put one hundred silver dollars on the table and we arranged them to form the letters "W o W," standing for Word of Wisdom. After taking a picture of him standing proudly by his reward money, off he went.

Where did he go? Worthily, on a mission to Taiwan. Worthily, to the temple to be sealed to his bride. Brad and his wife, Cindy, now have three marvelous children, the eldest of whom is Tyler. And when Tyler—who was my one and only great-nephew at that point—was about six years old, I took him aside and asked him what he knew about the Lord's "law of health." You can complete the rest of that story.

Now let's go back to the words on the old barn roof!

Think about

What do you think the words were?

If you could write any three words on your roof, on a T-shirt or banner, stencil them on a sign, or cross-stitch them on a pillow to help others live a better life, what three words would you choose? What three words would help you the most?

Are you ready for the great unveiling of the three words? Drum roll, please.

The three words were . . .

NOT
EVEN
ONCE

Just imagine if that were the motto by which you lived your life! Imagine what would happen if you were to determine that from this moment on, there are certain things you will never do—or never do again . . .

From this moment on—you would never

Break the Word of Wisdom • Lie • Cheat • Steal • Gossip • Procrastinate • Dress immodestly • Break the law of chastity—in any way

Look at anything pornographic—on TV, the Internet, your cell phone, billboards, magazines, in movies[1]

NOT EVEN ONCE

Not Even Once

Think about

Is there something you would like to overcome in your life? Are you ready to make a commitment that you will never again surrender to it—

NOT EVEN ONCE?

Write about

Try to imagine how you would feel if you were to apply the NOT EVEN ONCE rule to some weakness or behavior that is robbing you of peace and the companionship of the Holy Ghost.

- Write down the difference it would make in your life to be free of that thing.
- How would it change your relationship with someone you love?
- How would your experience at Church change?
- How would your prayers change?
- Even your sleep—how would it change?

Write about how the NOT EVEN ONCE rule could help you in your life—right now—from this moment on—and forever.

One healthy, trim, and lovely young woman shared with me her NOT EVEN ONCE story. Although she had never seen the three words on the old barn roof, nor heard the story, she had lived her life regarding one food item as though she had.

When she was about nine years of age, she noticed that she was gaining weight. And she noticed what she was eating: lots and lots of chocolate. She noticed as well that some of her family members were also gaining weight. And they were eating lots and lots of chocolate, too. So, at the young age of nine, she made a decision that she would never eat chocolate again! And for over a decade she hasn't. Not even once! She recently married, and among the many assets she is bringing to her marriage are the joy and strength of character that comes to one who makes a commitment and keeps it.

A courageous Hawaiian woman told me the amazing benefits she gained by observing the NOT EVEN ONCE rule when she applied it to refined sugar. Again, she had not seen the barn, but she had resolved that because of present and prospective health problems, she had to avoid refined sugar at all costs. Impeccably. She did, and within a year she lost over one hundred pounds and gained her health and a brand-new life! All because she was true to her determination.

Now, there are those among us, present company included, who have not had the strength to keep a commitment regarding some food items. Let me give you, unfortunately, a personal example:

For one full year I lived by a decision I made to avoid eating refined sugar. As I succeeded in keeping that commitment to myself, it was a great feeling. I was enjoying the many benefits that come with good health. My husband had been very helpful in telling me early in our marriage, as we went to yet another food-laced social gathering, "Just because they offer it doesn't mean you have to eat it." I felt freed up not to eat Aunt Gertie's lemon pie, which she had made especially for our visit and, amazingly, no one seemed offended that I didn't inhale the delicacy.

However, very late one night (can you feel the gloom gathering?), surrounded by friends and away from home and at the end of a very long and successful event where I had given my all, one of my friends pulled out a chocolate cake. My knee-jerk reaction after a year of saying "No, thank you" was to say, "No, thank you." Which I did. However, the friend persisted. "Oh, Wendy, you've been so good for an entire year. Just have a little piece. Just this once."

Well, sadly, instead of responding NOT EVEN ONCE, I responded by having one small piece. And then another. Several of us nibbled away at the huge chocolate cake.

I entitled this picture "1:00 A.M" because that's when I came to my senses and took this photograph. Many of us know the grief of those 1:00 A.M. moments when we realize what we have done. When we realize we've just broken our NOT EVEN ONCE rule.

What do we do then?

The adversary loves to whisper to you that you've blown it and you're a loser and there is no use doing anything but to keep breaking the rule you said you would never break.

But what can we do?
What should we do?

We can grieve. We can repent. We can ask the Lord for His forgiveness. And, depending upon the seriousness of our 1:00 A.M. experience, we may need the help of our priesthood leaders to fully repent, to access the cleansing, healing power of the Savior's Atonement, and to start living our lives by the NOT EVEN ONCE rule again.

It is not easy. It is not without struggle and anguish and lots of persistent effort for a prolonged period of time on our part, but with the Savior's help and His power, it can be as though that 1:00 A.M. moment never happened and you can resume living your NOT EVEN ONCE rule. How thrilling is that? So much more thrilling than that taste of chocolate cake!

Now let's go back to the NOT EVEN ONCE rule.

I had the privilege of telling several hundred school children in Samoa about the three words on that old barn roof. They were sitting on the floor of the gathering room in their school and they were captivated by this concept.

The children spontaneously chimed in with me every time I would say *"Not even once"*—over and over again, throughout the telling of the story. I was moved almost to tears to hear these young children have such a desire to speak truth, to repeat truth, to declare a determination that will help them in the days ahead.

A few days later, on that same trip to the South Pacific on assignment with my husband, I told the story to the students at the Church College in New Zealand. One young student took the experience to heart and wrote her feelings down in the following poem:

Not Even Once E. R. LOLO

Everyone's doing it
Just once is okay
These beguiling words
We face each day.

When faced with temptation
Do I falter or waver?
Will the Lord excuse
A little sinful behavior?

The Lord loves me
Then why should I doubt?
Though devils assail and
Their successes they tout.

Pluck up your courage
And today begin
To follow the Lord
NOT the author of sin.

Everyone's doing it
What sorrow that brings
Stand strong in the truth
My faith gives me wings.

I will fly above
All that is sin and vice
I won't give in once
For that leads to twice.

NOT EVEN ONCE!
Is the clarion call
Remember this always
Walk strong and tall.[2]

YOU CAN ALSO APPLY THE *NOT EVEN ONCE* RULE TO POSITIVE THINGS. THINGS YOU NEVER WANT TO MISS AN OPPORTUNITY TO DO—NOT EVEN ONCE. FOR EXAMPLE:

To NOT EVEN ONCE miss an opportunity

- to forgive someone—someone who may never repent and who will probably never apologize to you for the pain they have caused.
- to fully repent—so that you can be freed from emotional pain and know that the Lord will never remember your sins.
- to take a question to the scriptures daily.
- to be kinder than you need to be—especially to someone who isn't.
- to pay a full tithing.
- to serve and worship in the temple and claim the promised powers and blessings.
- to really listen and participate in your mind and heart as the sacrament prayers are spoken so that you are truly renewing your baptismal covenants, and in the process become renewed.
- to fast with a purpose.
- to pray with faith, beseeching Heavenly Father, in the name of Jesus Christ, for those things you really need.
- to pray for opportunities to share your love of the restored gospel of Jesus Christ and to be ready with a short, engaging response to accompany the pass-along card and Book of Mormon you carry.
- to ______________ (how would you fill in that blank?)

Write about

Those things that you never want to miss an opportunity to do—
from this moment on—NOT EVEN ONCE.

What can happen as we take this approach to our lives?

Wonderful things!

Marvelous things!

As you make—and keep—
a commitment to yourself
and to the Lord
that there are certain things
you will not do
from this moment on,
you will be able to do
all that you committed
premortally to do.

That's a promise.

And you'll be happy!
And you'll be more of your true self!

Now for an update

Remember my little great-nephew Tyler, who at age six enrolled in the Word of Wisdom agreement with me? Well, when he was eight years old I told him the story about the NOT EVEN ONCE sign. He was fascinated by the three words and said, "Aunt Wendy, that's the motto I'm going to live my life by."

On Tyler's ninth birthday, I had the opportunity to be with him and several of his cousins—my great-nieces and great-nephews. Tyler helped me tell the other children the story about the old barn, the three words, and about the Word of Wisdom agreement, complete with the one-hundred-dollar promise.

All the children were thoroughly engaged and readily enlisted in the NOT EVEN ONCE Club. They went marching up the stairs to their parents, chanting their new motto: NOT EVEN ONCE!

I was struck by the enthusiastic response of these children and wondered if I were seeing through their actions how our spirits feel in the presence of truth and firm determinations and declarations. Our spirits long for the freedom and the peace, the joy and the thrill, of living our lives according to the NOT EVEN ONCE! rule.

That's what making and keeping sacred covenants with the Lord is all about!

Let us live so that the words written in Alma 57:21 will be said about us:

"They did obey and observe to perform every word of command with exactness."

Try It

Pray to know how the Lord would have you answer the following question, which can change your life:

*What commitment am I willing to make to the Lord and to myself, that **I will never do,** or never do again, from this moment on— **not even once?***

And pray to know how the Lord would want to you answer this question:

*What commitment am I willing to make to the Lord and to myself, **that I will never miss an opportunity to do** from this moment on— **not even once?***

QUESTION #4

WHOSE AGENDA IS THIS SUPPORTING?

"Why are you throwing out all those videotapes, honey?"

That's the question a woman asked her husband as he struggled to balance a huge stack of movie videotapes he was carrying out to the trash. She actually wanted to say, "Well, it's about time!" but something restrained her.

She was both stunned and thrilled by what he was doing. She had been concerned for such a long time about the movies he watched—even though by the world's standards they were tame. Just the week before, the two had talked about what they could do to make their home a better place, filled with peace and love. At that point, he had reluctantly parted with six of his movies, but she continued to be concerned about the influence the remaining movies were having on her husband's heart and mind—and on their home.

She didn't want to be a nag so she poured her heart out to her Father in Heaven: "Please help my husband remove any videotapes that are preventing the Spirit from being in our home—in full abundance." What an important tag line: **in full abundance**.

That had been a few days before, and now here he was, heading for the garbage can with a stack of movies he could barely carry and saying that there were more he was throwing away! So she asked the question: "Why are you throwing out all those videotapes, honey?"

His answer?

"A question kept coming to my mind and I used it to evaluate all my movies."

What was the question?

Whose agenda is this supporting?

He threw out any movie that he determined was supporting the adversary's agenda.

And in doing so, he threw out every movie that was preventing the Spirit from being in the home—**in full abundance!**

Whose agenda is this supporting?

What a great question to use when making any decision—even in the seemingly small choices we make every day. For example, do we consider that clothing that is too tight, too low, too short, or too revealing supports the adversary's agenda?

Whose agenda is it supporting when we become casual in the clothes we wear to Church?

Elder Jeffrey R. Holland mentored the young women and their mothers when he said,

"I make a special appeal regarding how young women might dress for Church services and Sabbath worship. . . . Our clothing or footwear need never be expensive, indeed should not *be expensive, but neither should it appear that we are on our way to the beach."*[1]

How touching it was when my husband and I attended church in Nigeria and Mozambique and witnessed our LDS young women and their mothers following this counsel and dressing for church as though they were truly going to worship the Lord.

Whose agenda is this supporting?

What a great question to use as we make decisions about everything we do, say, think, and feel!

WHOSE AGENDA ARE WE SUPPORTING IF WE:

- Whine and complain about our lot in life—but do nothing to improve it by drawing closer to the Lord to seek His guidance
- Take offense at everything
- Fail to give others the benefit of the doubt
- Focus on how much no one seems to be focusing on us
- Lie a little
- Cheat a little
- Steal a little
- Break the laws of the land and set a crippling example for our children—and future generations—to do the same
- Sneak a peek at pornography—just a little—and deceive ourselves that it doesn't hurt anyone, and become blind to the ravaging effect pornography is slowly but surely having upon our spirits and bodies
- Dress in such a manner that we "become pornography"[2]
- Dress to resemble a woman of the world rather than a woman of God
- Act as a man of the world rather than as a man of God
- Lust—just a little
- Covet—a lot! —everything that is advertised on billboards and on TV and on the Internet, not to mention everything your neighbor owns
- Deny that we are doing any of those things, yet keep on doing them
- Mismanage our finances in such a way that we are held hostage by the demon of debt
- Are easily swayed by the latest fashions and theories of "the world"

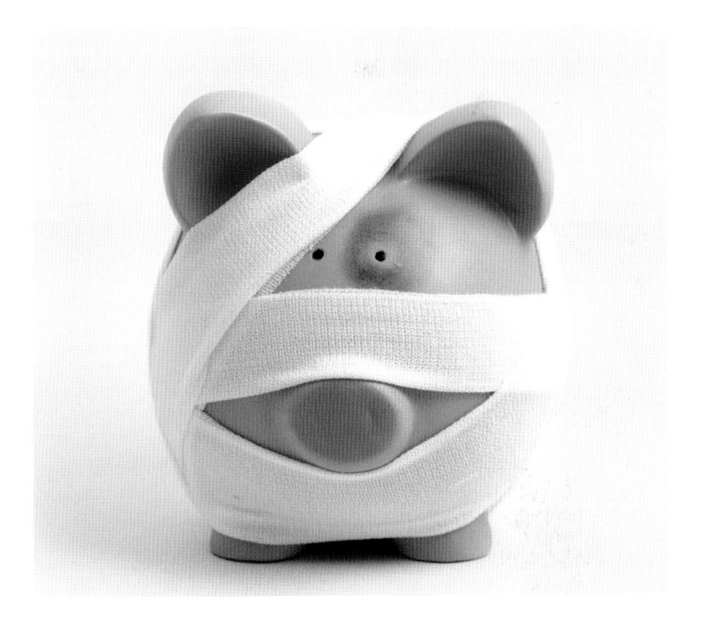

WHOSE AGENDA ARE WE SUPPORTING IF WE:

- Look to "the world" to tell us where we should be spending our time, energy, and money
- Focus on the mistakes of others
- Always find someone or something to blame for our own mistakes
- Spend hours in front of the TV or on recreational Internet Web sites or playing video games
- Seek pleasure and try at all costs to avoid pain—any kind of pain
- Inflict pain upon others—all kinds of pain
- Fail to see how much a family member needs our love and support
- Offer love for a time to someone in need, but fail to offer the truths of the restored gospel of Jesus Christ, which would help them forever
- Withhold our support of another's life's mission and success
- Are cruel in our comments about others—to their face or behind their backs
- Withhold our appreciation and affection from others
- Hold a grudge
- Partake of the sacrament casually so that it becomes more a Sunday ritual than a sacred binding ordinance complete with our sincere honoring of the covenant
- Fail to find time to feast on the words of Christ, but always find time to feast upon everything that falls from the lips of politicians, celebrities, rock stars, scholars, and pundits
- Care more about being politically correct in our statements about marriage and family and life and love than about being true disciples of the Lord Jesus Christ

- Plan our day so we won't miss the next episode of a TV show, but fail to plan our lives so there is regular immersion in temple worship and service
- Always find time to do whatever we really want to do, but never quite find time to do what the Lord needs us to do
- Care more about how other people see us than about how the Lord sees us
- Fear what men and women can do to us
- Forget what the Lord has done for us and fail to seek what He will continue to do
- Try to hide our sins rather than repent
- Seek to gratify our pride and vanity
- Exercise unrighteous dominion in any way
- Fail to acknowledge the Lord's hand in all that we do
- Don't ask our Heavenly Father in the name of Jesus Christ for those things we desperately need in our lives

Write about

Now that you have read this noninclusive list of things that support the adversary's agenda, go back and read it one more time—this time writing down those things that may have crept into your life. Write down those things that you want to be increasingly aware of and that you want to stop doing so you will cease supporting the adversary's agenda.

Think about

Whose agenda are we supporting when we relax our spiritual muscles, don't do the spiritual work of asking and seeking, and thus live far beneath our privileges?

I wonder if, before we set off for our mortal experiences, one or two of us may have said to our Heavenly Father:

Oh, Heavenly Father, Thou art going to make this experience too easy. I thought this was going to be a test. Dost Thou mean Thou art going to give us an ability to talk to Thee anytime, to tell Thee what we need, and to receive help from Thee for the entire time we're on earth? Oh, that's going to make it so easy.

And Thou art willing to give us scriptures? Am I understanding this correctly? We can immerse our lives in the truths of eternity and have brought to our minds the truths we now know? Isn't that going to make the veil that Thou said would be put in place a bit too thin?

And Thou art going to give us prophets and apostles? Holy men single-mindedly devoted to Thee who will bring us the current messages from Thee for Thy Church and Kingdom on earth? Messages from Thee that will continue to keep us moving steadily through the obstacle course of mortal life and back home to Thee?

And Thou art going to give us temples? Sacred spaces in the midst of the corruption and filth of the world that will allow us to be in Thy presence and to make sacred covenants that will forever bind us to Thee and to those we love?

wooden signs—*Families Can Be Together Forever*—doesn't mean it will happen. Being together forever with our family is not a given reality, as resurrection is. Everyone will be resurrected. We don't have to do anything to receive that blessing except be born and die! However, to live with our families forever, to see our mother and father and children and sisters and nieces and uncles after we die, and be with them forever . . . well, that's a different story. We have to first live worthily in order to receive the ordinances, and then we have to keep our covenants with the Lord throughout our lives on earth by continuing to live worthily—which basically means living much differently from most people in the world.

Sweet sentiments about being with those you love forever have a place. Where is it? On greeting cards. But sweet sentiments won't get us back home, living with our Heavenly Parents and with those we love. We need the reality of righteous living and receiving the Lord's saving ordinances of baptism, endowment, and sealing to give us the power to back up the desires of our hearts.

Whose agenda are we supporting when we think that there is no need for God-given ordinances and covenants?

Whose agenda are we supporting when we believe we can act and think and work and play and dress and talk and live just like the rest of the world and still be worthy and ready to do what the Lord needs us to do, to have the true joy that our Father wants us to have here in this mortal life, to learn the lessons He would have us learn, and to return worthily to Him?

Whose agenda are we supporting when we buy into the lie that there is no devil? That he and his followers are not real and are not trying to do everything possible to distract us from our purpose and missions here upon the earth?

Whose agenda are we supporting when we are not on the lookout for every form of deception and derailment by the author of misery himself?

Think about

In what ways would your life be different if, before every decision you make—from what to wear, to what to do today; from which career to pursue as your life's work, to what movie to watch tonight; from which friends to associate with, to what to do with your money, time, and talents—you were to ask yourself:

If I do this, whose agenda am I supporting?

What would you notice, or even be drawn to do differently, if for the next twenty-four hours you used the following question on a moment-by-moment basis to review each and every one of your major and minor decisions of the day:

As I choose to . . .

do this,
say this,
watch this,
wear this,
read this,
write this,
pursue this,
believe this,
challenge this,
stand up for this,
remember this,
forget this,

whose agenda am I supporting?

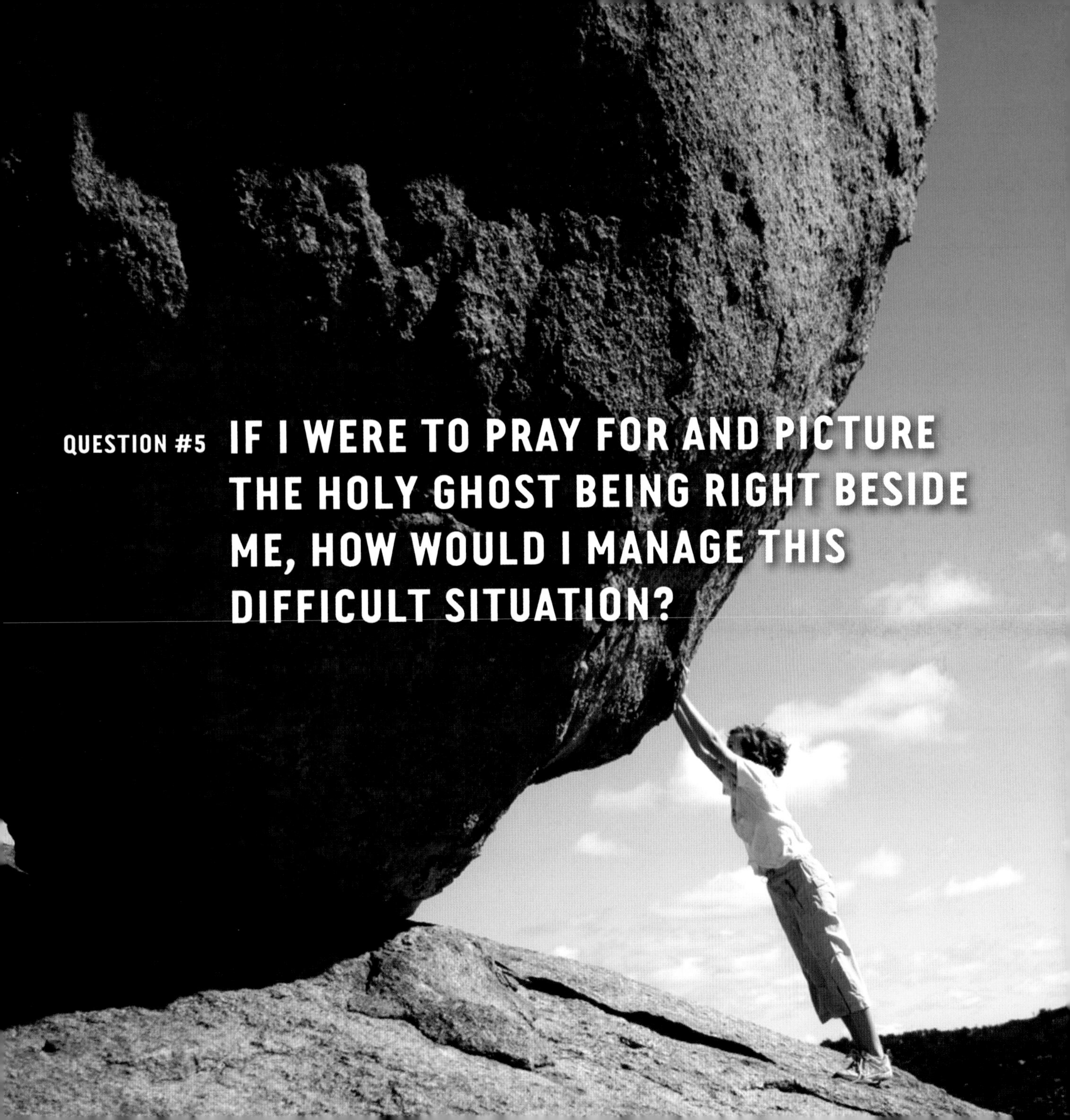
QUESTION #5
IF I WERE TO PRAY FOR AND PICTURE THE HOLY GHOST BEING RIGHT BESIDE ME, HOW WOULD I MANAGE THIS DIFFICULT SITUATION?

Think about

Think about the most difficult, trying, or tempting situation you have ever faced.

How did you manage it?

What did you do that helped?

What do you wish you had done differently?

I've thought a lot about a statement made by Brigham Young.
When speaking of how to manage difficult, trying, or tempting situations,
President Young said:

STOP

AND LET THE SPIRIT, WHICH GOD HAS PUT INTO YOUR TABERNACLES, TAKE THE LEAD.[1]

I love that!

Stop and let your spirit—complete with its divinely inherited DNA (so to speak) take the lead.

Let your spirit, under the direction of the Holy Ghost, respond to the situation.

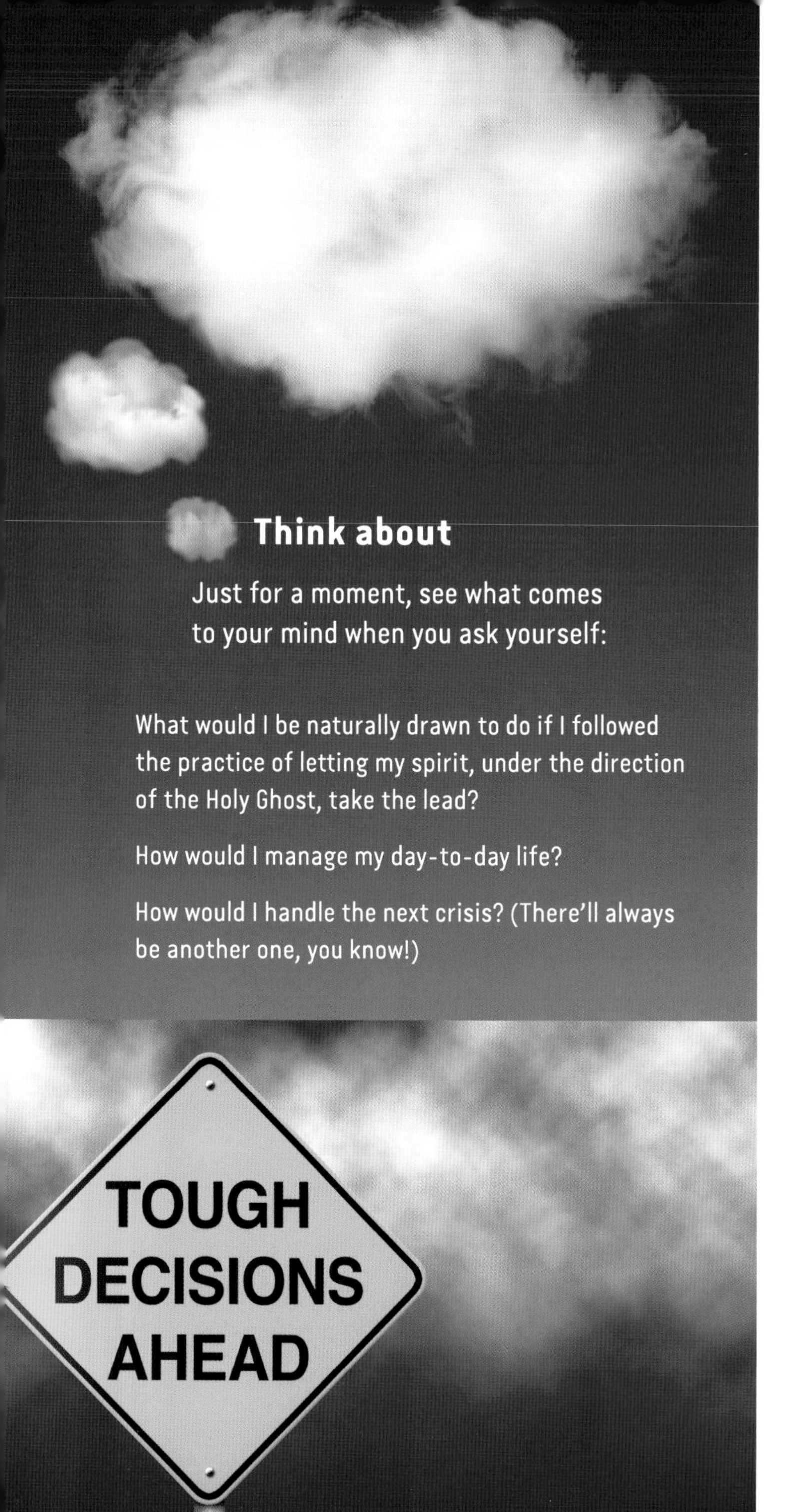

What would you be able to do, say, think, or feel with the Holy Ghost right by your side?

We are given the gift of the Holy Ghost's companionship when we are confirmed a member of The Church of Jesus Christ of Latter-day Saints. The third member of the Godhead can be right there with us as we live worthily and pray for His help and companionship. Imagine that privilege!

I remember a day when I recognized the reality of the companionship of the Holy Ghost. A wonderful young woman had called to ask if she could meet with me. She was a returned missionary—bright, capable, competent, faithful. Pick an adjective that would describe a virtuous and lovely young Latter-day Saint woman, and you would have Barbara (not her real name) described to a T. As part of my normal preparation for our meeting, I prayed before she arrived that the Spirit might guide our conversation.

Barbara wanted to talk about a tough situation in her life: the upcoming wedding of her younger brother. She was single and had not really dated since returning from her mission, and that posed a huge problem in her mind. Having her younger brother getting married made it even worse.

Her story went something like this:

"I just don't know what to do. I love my brother and want to support him. But the thought of going to his wedding is really difficult for me. I know as soon as I go home, all the people in my town and ward and stake will be there, and seeing them is just going to be awful. My Laurel adviser will ask if I am dating anyone! Ugh! I just hate the thought of being the sweet little returned missionary—the pathetic older sister—who isn't dating.

"Should I go? Should I take a date? There's a guy I'm kind of seeing. We're really just friends. I guess I could ask him, but then again I don't want to give him the wrong message when we're not really "dating." How horrible to take a guy-friend to the wedding of your brother with all the family there? I can just imagine all the conversations that will take place behind his back about 'Do you think this is the one for Barbara?'

"I don't know what to do. I actually did think of another plan—you'll think I'm really desperate—but I wondered if I should just hire someone to come with me. How creepy would

that be? I really don't want to go alone. I can't stand the thought of showing up at my baby brother's wedding all by myself. I wonder if I should even go at all. But then, how bad is that? Not even attend my brother's wedding? I can't not *go. But I really don't want to go alone. What should I do?"*

One other "little" detail would make her visit to her family for her brother's wedding even more difficult: It was all happening at Christmastime! A younger brother's wedding when you are single and not dating, with all the family and friends present, in your hometown—at Christmastime—is a recipe for intense dread!

After hearing Barbara's distress and her several ideas about a solution, none of which appealed to her, I found myself initiating a conversation about the reality of the Holy Ghost.

Had Barbara experienced the Holy Ghost in her life?

Of course. Many times.

She had felt that sweet companionship when teaching the gospel and had received a sure witness of the Spirit that what she was teaching was true. She had watched that same assurance come upon investigators as they listened. She had recently felt prompted by the Spirit to take a new job even though the salary was much less than she had been making at her previous employment.

Yes, Barbara knew the Holy Ghost had directed her in her life from time to time and had brought the truths of the gospel to her mind many times. She knew He could bring comfort, although she really hadn't had that experience. And she knew the blessing found in the sacrament prayers—*"that they may always have his Spirit to be with them"* (Moroni 4:3; see also 5:2)—was real and true.

Then I shifted our conversation and asked her to describe in detail a couple of the situations that might arise as part of her brother's wedding.

She said, "Well, first there's the social in the cultural hall the night before the temple wedding, where all the family and friends will gather."

I stopped her.

"Okay, Barbara. Just for a moment, picture the Holy Ghost being right there by you in that setting. Picture the Spirit of the Lord, the Holy Ghost, the third member of the Godhead being by your side, being your companion for this important family time."

She was a little taken aback.

"You've experienced His companionship since you were eight years old, so just relax and close your eyes for a moment. Visualize in your mind's eye the cultural hall. See your Laurel adviser and picture the Holy Ghost by your side."

Barbara did so. She started to breathe differently and smile, just slightly. I watched the tension and stress and fear drain away from her face and body.

I invited her to go deeper. "Tell me how you would prepare yourself for seeing your Laurel adviser—with the Holy Ghost as your companion. What would you wear? How would you look? How would you stand, smile, walk? What would you talk about—knowing that the Holy Ghost was right there by your side?"

She was able to describe the scene in great detail. She said she would be smiling, relaxed, excited to see people—with Him right there with her. She would stand tall, and she knew what she would wear that would make her feel comfortable and lovely. She would take an interest in other people and not worry about herself. She basically described the confidence—in speech, in action, in thought and feeling—that comes when we know the Spirit is with us.

We spent the rest of our time together going through several more situations. How would things be in the temple sealing room? Where would she sit? How would she feel? How would she behave toward her mother, her father, her brother, his bride—knowing that the Holy Ghost was right there with her?

Then, how would she respond as pictures would be taken, knowing that she was *not* alone? And how would she feel at the wedding reception with all the guests and the tributes—again knowing that *her* companion was the Spirit of the Lord?

Our conversation was a remarkable experience for both of us. She, peeking into the future, seeing events unfold with the Holy Ghost right there with her. I, having the privilege to observe the dramatic difference made by both the prospect, and the reality, of the companionship of the Holy Ghost. There was no doubt for either Barbara or me that the Holy Ghost had been our companion throughout that important conversation.

Barbara left our meeting a different young woman than when she arrived. She was more relaxed and much more confident. She even looked different! She was now even a bit excited about the adventure ahead. She was going to pray for the Spirit to be with her, and she was going to picture Him right there by her side through each and every moment until her return to Salt Lake City after Christmas.

I still remember the e-mail I received from Barbara a few weeks later. She wrote:

"I couldn't wait to get back to Salt Lake so I could send you this e-mail and tell you about my time at home. I had the best time I've ever had with my family and friends. I could feel the Holy Ghost being right there with me in every situation.

"I was able to be my true self. I loved being with my baby brother and was so proud of him. I laughed and cried—appropriately. It was truly the most wonderful time I think I've ever had at home—all because I knew the Spirit of the Lord was with me.

"I am so grateful I had an opportunity to think deeply about what 'the constant companionship of the Holy Ghost' really means and that, if I wanted, the Holy Ghost could literally be with me throughout the wedding events. I was most concerned about being alone in the temple sealing room, but I knew it was possible to have Him sitting right next to me. I prayerfully made the request that I have an awareness, like I had never had before, that the Holy Ghost was indeed with me.

"For as long as I live, I will never forget that day. I walked into that sealing room confident. Confident in the knowledge that I was not alone. I remember sitting down and although there was not an empty chair next to me, I felt the physical presence of the third member of the Godhead! The Holy Ghost was literally my companion that day. He sat with me in the sealing room and He accompanied me to the wedding lunch and reception later in the day. I knew that day, in a way that I hadn't known before, that my Father in Heaven and my Savior really really really *love me. I also knew that the companionship of the Spirit is not just a nice concept, but rather a literal promise."*

The Five-Day Experiment

How would you handle the very next situation in your life if you prayed for and pictured the Holy Ghost being right there with you?

Building upon Barbara's experience, I wondered what other women could learn and teach us from a five-day experiment: eight women ranging in age from 18 to 55 and in all stages of life—university student, single and working, married and working, married with young children, married with adult "launched" children, grandmother.

And what was the five-day experiment?

For five days, each of these eight women was to pray in her morning prayers with concerted effort for the Holy Ghost to be with her that day. (Now, that's nothing new. That's what most of us do all the time.)

But then, *throughout* the day, as they encountered *any* difficult, tempting, or trying situation—*right in that moment*—they were to pray for and really picture the Spirit being right there with them.

The resulting experiences of these women blew us all away! They came to know for themselves—in an incredibly short amount of time and in very tangible ways—the truth of Nephi's words when he said,

"The Holy Ghost . . . will show unto you all things what ye should do" *(2 Nephi 32:5).*

My friends had no doubt about that after five short days!

Think about

- What would you be naturally drawn to do with the Holy Ghost by your side?
- What would you have more courage to say or not say?
- Where would you choose to spend your time—if you prayed for the Spirit, imagined Him, even pictured Him being right there with you?
- What projects would you approach differently?
- What problems would fall away with Him by your side?

Do you know that the Holy Ghost loves cleanliness?

One of the very first things each of these women reported was a great desire to clean up their homes. To dejunk. To clear away the debris. To spruce up, clean up, toss out. To do everything they could to clean and simplify and beautify their physical environments.

I hadn't told them to go home and clean out their basements and garages, but just picturing the Holy Ghost being right there with them prompted these women to do just that.

Their experience reminded me of what a stake patriarch in California taught me years ago. I was traveling with him and his wife to an event, and I took the opportunity to ask him, *"How do you prepare to give a patriarchal blessing?"*

I was anticipating that he would tell me something such as, *"I review the names of the twelve tribes of Israel. I read Isaiah. I read Abraham. I fast. I pray."*

Now, he may do all of those things, but what he told me that evening was, *"I start by vacuuming the room!"*

I love that answer!

In a meeting held a few years later and in another state, I shared the patriarch's answer and the experience of the eight women. Following the meeting, the stake president said to me, "Wendy, what you taught tonight is true." (That's always a relief to hear.)

He said, "I want you to come with me to our high council room." It was just across the hall from the chapel. When he turned on the lights, he said, "When we have the privilege of holding a disciplinary council here, we make sure there isn't one extra chair or hymnal or piece of paper in this room. We want to make sure there isn't anything that will prevent the Spirit of the Lord being with us."

Think about

When you pray for and picture the Holy Ghost being right by your side, what do you feel compelled to clean up, or clear away, in your physical environment?

What else did the eight women learn?

Each of them felt a greatly reduced desire to watch TV. They didn't want to spend their time being mindlessly bombarded with whatever some twenty-four-year-old TV executive decided was "prime." The university student said, *"I just didn't feel like watching that 'Friendly' show."*

They also reported an increased desire to reach out to others and to follow through on commitments they had made to the Lord, to others, and to themselves.

With the Holy Ghost as their companion, they experienced an increased ability to be kinder, gentler, more patient. They were amazed by how much their abilities in these areas increased in such a short time.

A young wife and mother said, *"I wasn't aware that my three-year-old noticed how calmly I handled a situation that normally would have aggravated me. 'Mom,' my daughter said, with a mix of surprise and gratitude, 'you have* good *patience!'"*

These women also had an increased desire to take care of their bodies by living the Lord's law of health more fully. One woman reported that she started thinking much *more* about life and much *less* about food, and that made all the difference!

With the third member of the Godhead right there with them, these women quickly saw how they could have handled a situation better—including "mothering moments" that went awry! There seemed to be an instant feedback mechanism available to them.

They had an increased mental focus and an increased ability and desire to really study and learn. They wanted to seek, to study, to use their minds. This was an exhilarating feeling for each of them—even for those who were presently attending a university or were avid readers. There was something different about this feeling. An expanded desire. More excitement. Almost an insatiable urge to take in knowledge. To think. Perhaps they were feeling some of the truth: *"The glory of God is intelligence"* (D&C 93:36).

These women found that old tendencies to backbite, gossip, or speak critically of others lost their appeal. There was no compulsion to let others know that they were up on the latest news in another's life. There was also no need to talk about "connections" to all those "really special people" out there. They had more important things to do than drop names. They felt a true desire to be about their *Father's* business, rather than be into everyone else's business.

They described a dramatic increase in their physical energy because energy draining negative emotions were gone. One said, *"In the evening I actually felt like cleaning up my home, and my husband and I started running together after work. What a change from sitting, exhausted, with him in front of the TV and complaining about my day—all night!"*

A shift in priorities occurred. One reported, *"For our date night, we chose to go to the temple instead of to a movie."*

And—note this—they experienced an unbelievable reduction in stress. One young mother of two children, both under the age of three, said, *"The* pace *of my days changed. Everything got done, yet without my usual franticness. Everything was more peaceful, more meaningful."*

The women also experienced profound changes in their conversations with others.

They told me that their very best advice to others would be, *"Don't have* any *conversation without the Holy Ghost."*

Commenting on this, the first-year university student said, *"I felt more confident with people. I listened in a different way to my friends, and I knew how to respond to those who were having problems. It was as though I knew what I said was true, and so did they."*

A middle-aged mother and grandmother said, *"I was able to express some concerns to my husband in a way that he could really hear them. Usually, when I've tried in the past, I'm either too emotional or I soft-pedal the whole thing because I don't want to upset him. In either case, I'm not taken seriously. This time, with the Spirit with me, I had a voice. It was as though the Holy Ghost gave me my voice. I felt empowered—although that's not quite the right word.*

"I had a clarity of thought and a clarity of expression that was beyond me. In fact, when I look back on the situation I think: 'That wasn't me'—and yet—I've never felt more like myself."

One woman experienced the Spirit helping her to know what *not* to say! She said, *"A colleague had been rather rude to me the day before but this day, really thinking about the Spirit being with me, I didn't feel any irritation. No malice. I also didn't feel like punishing him with either sarcasm or cold silence. He came to me and apologized, and I felt very calm. I felt as though I should just listen and be silent. It was like I was being taught how to 'be still' inside and out. Actually, I believe I was being taught how to be more Christlike, both in my actions and my feelings."*

A young wife and mother said, *"I felt as though I was taught to be more mindful of timing when I want to discuss things with my husband. I now see that, in the past, I've almost set us up for failure—for being frustrated with each other—by not being aware of how important timing is."*

Isn't it amazing what just five days of praying for and picturing the Holy Ghost being with them did for these women? Can you believe all that they learned? What they felt drawn to do? What they stopped doing? How their thoughts and feelings and conversations and actions changed—in just five days? If you ever wonder about the reality and the power of the Holy Ghost, think about these eight women and their five-day experiment.

And think about Barbara.

Better yet . . . **try it for yourself!**

Try it

For five days, in your morning prayers, pray with concerted effort, and with the faith of a child, for the Holy Ghost to be with you that day.

Then throughout the day

as you encounter any difficult, tempting, or trying situation—

right in that moment—

pray for and really picture

the Holy Ghost

being right there with you!

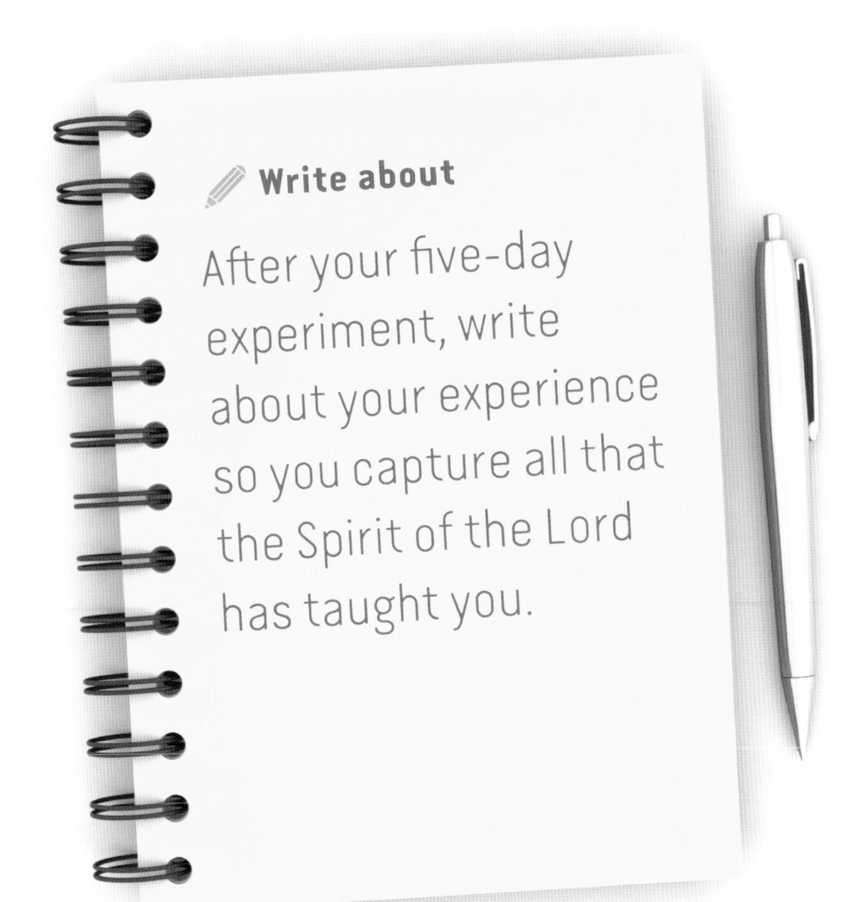

And, in the future, use the following question as a tool to help you whenever you need it.

IF I WERE TO PRAY FOR AND PICTURE
THE HOLY GHOST BEING RIGHT BESIDE ME,
HOW WOULD I MANAGE
THIS DIFFICULT SITUATION?

THAT QUESTION CAN CHANGE YOUR LIFE!

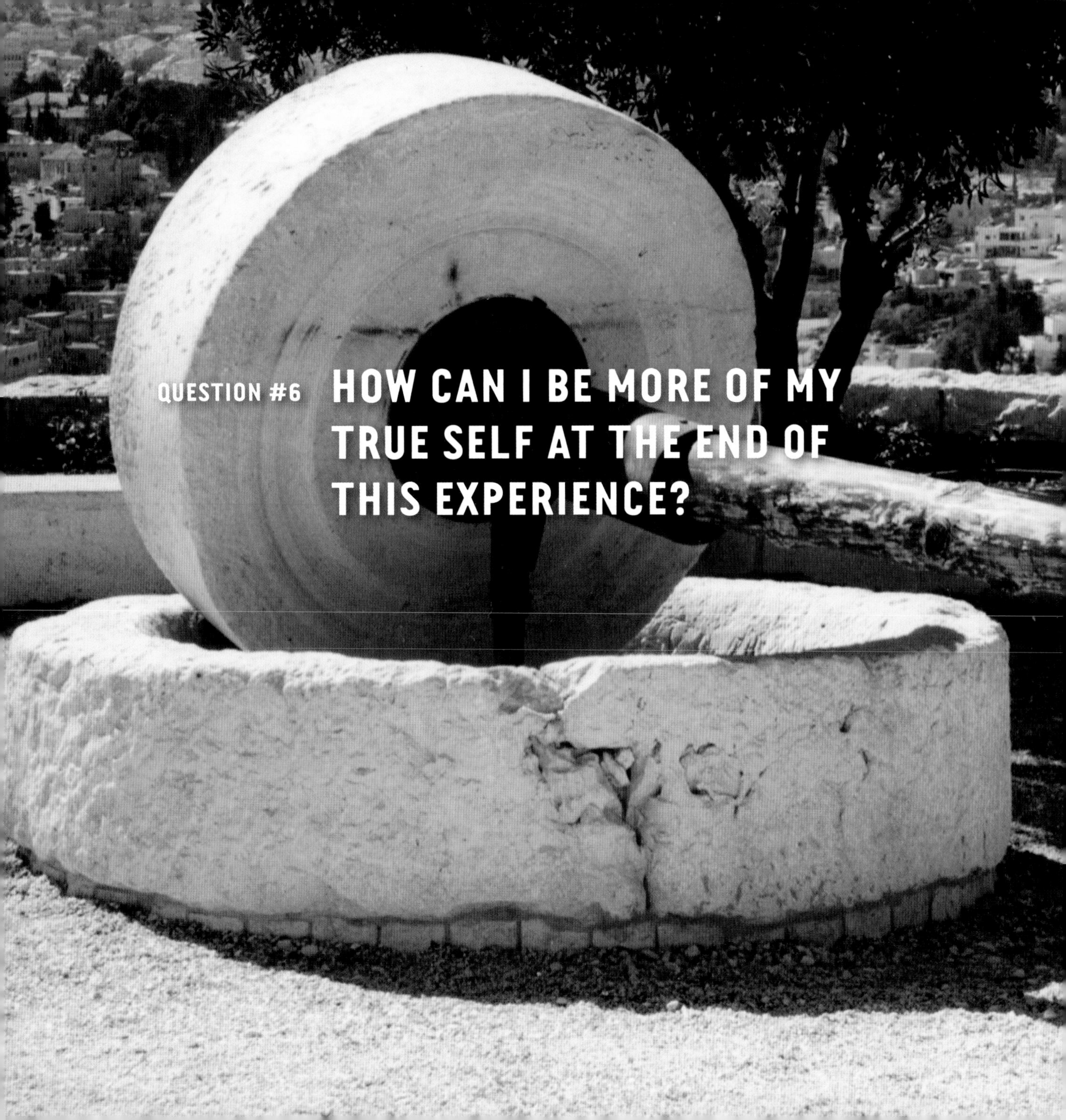

QUESTION #6

HOW CAN I BE MORE OF MY TRUE SELF AT THE END OF THIS EXPERIENCE?

It's pretty safe to say that at some point in your life, you will face a problem you never expected.

How will you handle it?

Will you handle it as your true self: courageous, determined, and filled with light? Or as a very "unreasonable facsimile" of yourself: pathetic, self-centered, and miserable?

Do you know who you are:

- when the pressure is mounting all around you?
- when people you love betray you?
- when false accusations are thrown at you?
- when all the former "givens" in your life can no longer be counted on?
- when a horrendous situation threatens to engulf and entrap you?

At those critical junctures, do you know who you *really* are?

The Lord expects you to live your life fully—even the unexpected life.

Why? Because facing the unexpected things in our lives and learning to manage them—perhaps even conquer them, rather than having them conquer us—can actually help us become more and more of our true selves. Does that sound impossible? That is what our lives are *for.*

"Life is a spook alley"[1]

You never know what is just around the bend or hiding in the corners. Or who is walking through your front door. You never know which people disguised as friends may turn out to be enemies to your true self, introducing you to all kinds of false philosophies and worldly practices—all in the name of friendship.

We need protective spiritual clothing if we are going to come out of this life spiritually alive. To survive, we need the very best there is. We need the full armor of God (Ephesians 6:11). And we need protective spiritual eyewear, namely, the spirit of discernment to see when a situation is unsafe or a person is not what they say they are.

Life is indeed a spook alley, but one in which we are supposed to grow more and more into our true selves!

I have the privilege of meeting many people around the world in various difficult life situations. And as these people, mostly women, speak to me in a very personal way, I am struck with the thought that *whatever* the horrendous, hideous, heart-wrenching, head-banging, spook-alley situation we may be in, what really matters is that we grow more and more into our true selves.

This is not to downplay the rigors of so many grueling situations we may find ourselves in, but if we are moving toward knowing and becoming more and more of who we really are—and, as Sheri Dew has taught, "who we have always been"[2]—what else really matters? Our pain and suffering and heartaches and fear can be taken from us by the Savior Himself. And He *will*. All we need to do is ask.

Write about

Write about one really difficult situation in your life that you survived. What helped? What did you learn about your

true self

from that experience?

How can we grow more into our true selves? Let me offer five principles:

Principle #1: Remove every obstacle that is preventing you from being your true self.

"You're not even like yourself anymore!" That's what her mother, in total despair, said to Carol one day. The mother had for many years watched her daughter suffer within a very demeaning marriage, and she could bear it no more. Her mother's words caught Carol's attention like nothing else had. She knew something drastic needed to happen. Carol and her mother prayed as they had never prayed before that the obstacle of Carol's torturous marriage could be removed. In the process of seeking help from the Lord, Carol became more and more of her true self. And in a most miraculous series of events—too sacred to speak about—the situation resolved itself. Each event evidenced the hand of the Lord. The obstacle was completely, totally, and thoroughly removed. And Carol arose as her true self once again.

Another woman finally found the courage and determination to tackle a lifelong weight problem, which she realized was becoming an obstacle to her being her true self. In a quest to discover her true self, and through prayer, she developed the strength to resist foods that made her body unhealthy, weak, and tired and thus she found the energy and ability to exercise. What a concept! She wanted to *look* more and more like her true self in order to *be* more and more like her true self. And she knew that her spirit was not life-threateningly overweight!

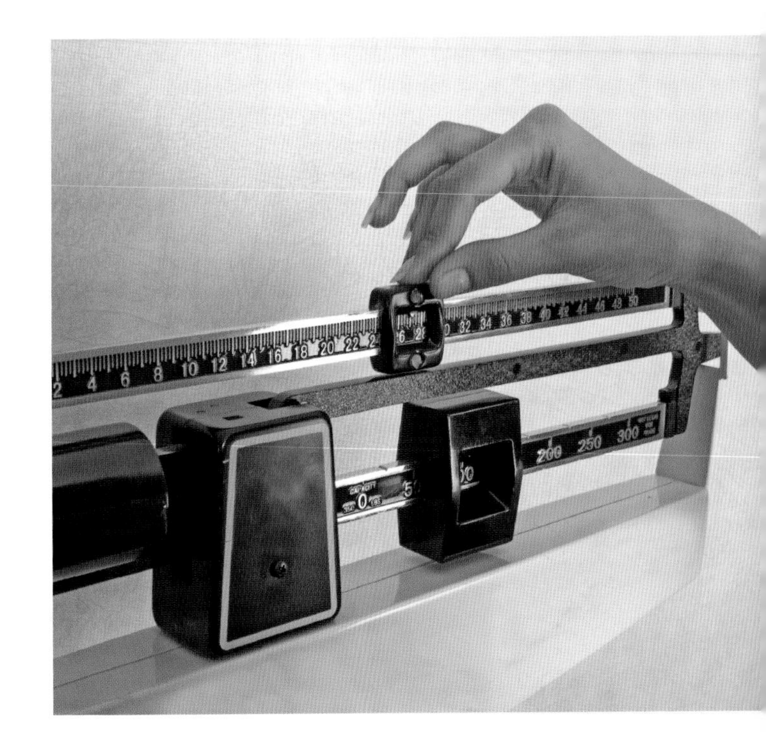

It may be important to utter this prayer from time to time:

Please remove every obstacle so that I can be my true self.

My great-great-grandmother Sarah had a deep desire to join the Church. Her husband, Ephraim, had also read the Book of Mormon and received a witness that it was true, but had been cautioned by his niece that if they joined the Church no one would patronize his business in their little Iowa town and the business would fail. Ephraim told Sarah that therefore he had decided not to join the Church. Sarah's response? "Well, Ephraim, you've made your decision. Now I'll make mine." Ephraim begged Sarah not to join, but Sarah could not turn away from what she knew to be true. She could not *not* join the Church. What could she do?

Every day she prayed fervently to the Lord for help so that she could join His Church. Time passed. Her pleadings continued. Ephraim's mandate that she not join the Church remained in place. Sarah felt like the heavens were made of brass, until one night she prayed in utter desperation a prayer that was a little different:

"***Please remove every obstacle*** *so that I can join The Church of Jesus Christ of Latter-day Saints.*"

That night her sons awakened her in the middle of the night saying, "Come quick, Mother. Father is dying. We have him downstairs in a tub of water trying to revive him."

As Sarah ran down the stairs to her dying husband, she remembered how she had prayed that night: "***Please remove every obstacle*** *so that I can join The Church of Jesus Christ of Latter-day Saints.*"

As soon as she remembered her prayer, she cried out loud, "Oh, no! Not like that!"

After he was revived, Ephaim told Sarah that in the very moment she cried out those words—"Oh, no! Not like that!"—that all the life which had been draining out of him, flowed back into him.

He then said to Sarah, "Were you praying that I would *die* so that you could join the Mormon Church?"

Sarah said, "No, I wasn't praying that you would die. But I was praying that every obstacle would be removed so that I *could* join."

Ephraim then said with great feeling to Sarah, "You can join the Church, but please don't pray like that anymore!"

There is power in prayer. There is power in praying to have obstacles removed that are preventing us from being our true selves.

Obstacles may be relationships that are blocking our progression. They may be addictions that hold us prisoner or resentments that eat away at the light and truths we know and that fill us with bitterness.

You can't be your true self if you are resentful. Here's the truth:

In a crucible-like situation, if you spend the entire time being resentful and bitter, you will be *less*, not more, of your true self at the end. And that would be more terrible than the situation you're in!

That glorious spirit of yours, that true essence of who you really are, will begin shrinking and become brittle—and it won't take much to break it. You will always feel as though you are just on the edge of "losing it."

I'VE BEEN STRUCK LATELY WITH JUST HOW RESENTFUL MANY OF US ARE.

One woman resents that her neighbor—who is not even close to being as spiritual and charitable as she herself is (or so she thinks)—was called to be the Relief Society president!

Another woman resents that her best friend can eat anything she wants and never gain a pound.

Still another resents that her abuser was not punished severely enough.

An embittered woman resents that her sister has been slacking off in helping with their aging parents. Another that her husband wouldn't let her have her hair in an updo for their wedding photos—twenty-five years ago!

One man resents that his children don't listen to his advice and that his daughter isn't married yet—or even dating!

Another disgruntled man resents that his house hasn't sold and that one of his clients has never paid his bill.

Still another resents that his mother died before he arrived at her bedside.

One cynical man resents that his friends are always in the limelight.

And one particularly unhappy woman resents that her brother never follows through on his commitments—ever!

Resentment is toxic!

It prevents us from feeling love.

It can stop us from experiencing light and truth because we don't seek for and can't fully enjoy the companionship of the Holy Ghost.

Yet it is when we are miserable, self-centered, and full of envy that we need the companionship of the Holy Ghost more than ever!

What can we do? Start with prayer.

When we let our Heavenly Father know that we want to—really want to—lay down our resentments, the Spirit comes to our aid. The Spirit can bring important things to our memories—such as our strengths—that we've been discounting.

The Holy Ghost can bring *all* things to our remembrance—not so we can continue to marinate our hearts in others' mistakes or brood about others' blunders—but so we can *finally* remove those destructive weapons of war from our hearts, one by one, and bury *each one* just as the converted Lamanites did.

As we look at each experience in the revealing light of the Holy Ghost—instead of through the dark shadows of the adversary—past experiences can look very different.

Our resentments can have far-reaching effects.

One man was horrified to discover that his unpredictable anger, generated by resentment, was having a terrifying effect on his four-year-old daughter. This innocent little girl had developed a morning routine of asking her older brother before going downstairs to breakfast, *"Is Daddy in a good mood today?"*

A woman learned that her teenage son suddenly moved out of their home because he didn't want to live one more moment anywhere that the Spirit didn't, and couldn't, reside. What was preventing the presence of the Holy Ghost in their home? His mother's relentless resentment toward his recently repentant father!

From what I have personally observed, resentment keeps us from enjoying the companionship of the Holy Spirit and leaves us so much more vulnerable to the buffetings of Satan. In fact, I believe that resentment is one of the adversary's most effective tools and that the emotions that accompany its bitterness can be more corrosive to our souls than things we might regard as much more serious sin.

You may be at a point in life where you feel relatively safe from temptations to be unchaste. And that may be so. But if Satan is powerless to entice you to behave immorally, he may be satisfied to entice you to be resentful. Make no mistake, Lucifer is the author of resentment, and he uses it to damage our souls and our relationships. Therefore, we need to identify the resentment we may be carrying around and get rid of it.

And to do so, we need the Spirit's supersleuthing skills.

What are some of the clues we might look for to discover where resentment may be hiding in our lives?

- Word jabs and barbs that slip out in our conversations or in our sarcastic comments.
- Disparaging remarks we make about others or the negative assumptions we make about why others behave as they do.
- Our inability to be happy for others' successes.
- Our inability to make decisions or to make the changes in our lives we so desperately need to make.

And resentment may even be behind our inability to really believe that there is power for us in the Atonement!

Think about

Is resentment hiding in your life?

Principle #2: Remember that you lived premortally.

Your true self came into being eons ago.

It has been revealed that the inhabitants of the earth are spiritually "begotten sons and daughters [of] God" (D&C 76:24). Prior to mortality we lived as spirit beings in the presence of our Heavenly Parents, for a very long period of time. We learned from them. We loved them, and we were loved by them. Established then was the essence of who we really are. That true essence resides in the spirits we brought to earth to receive our mortal bodies. When you are seeking to know who you really are—when you feel as though you are going through "an identity crisis" and don't know what to do—know this: You *are* a god or goddess in embryo!

Just as the DNA of your mortal parents resides in the cells of your mortal body, the divine "DNA" of your Heavenly Parents flows in the substance of your spirit body. If you don't take that truth into account as you are attempting to figure out your true identity, you will be forgetting the grandest and most fundamental truth about yourself.

As Dr. Allen Bergin, a pioneer in the field of modern psychotherapy, has so boldly stated:

"The human spirit, under God, is vital to understanding personality. . . . If we omit such spiritual realities from our account of human behavior, it won't matter much what else we keep in, because we will have omitted the most fundamental aspect of human nature."[3]

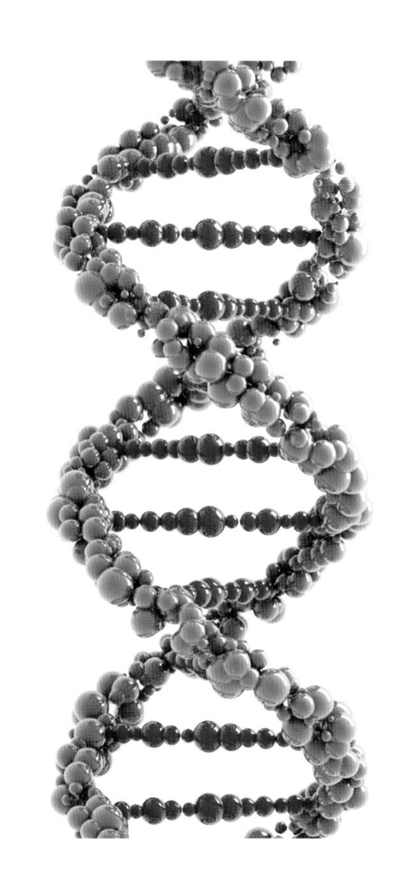

WHO AM I?

Who am I, this being that I am, who walks the earth midst beings as myself?
Born was I of parents; who are they?
Why do I exist to walk a while and then depart?
Who am I, who takes up time and space,
Who motions vacillate, some bad some good,
Who feels the null and void of all of this, without the question answered, who am I?

By happenchance have I come about by some ornate confusion?
By happenchance have I grown from rudimentary species eons past evolved?
By happenchance? By happenchance am I a worthless piece of thing
So dross, so void, so much of nothingness that when I pass,
My passing is just passing into past?
Who am I?

This is who I am!
My spirit lived with my Father before the earth was formed.
I chose the path to follow when my first estate was done.
I came to earth for a body created like my Father's;
To unite my spirit and body, to make my soul divine.
This is who I am! I am a child of my Father,
I am a child of my Father, My Father! My Father in Heaven.
This is who I am! I am a child, I am a child of God!
This is who I am.[4]

Write about

What comes to your mind when you consider the truths of your premortal life and identity?

Principle #3: You can be your true self only when you are obedient to the Lord and are near to Him.

In the midst of really difficult situations, we need to affirm our determination to be obedient to all that the Lord requires of us. And *before* really difficult situations occur, we need to draw closer to Him by being more obedient to His commandments!

Drawing near to the Lord is part of the process of finding our true selves. In fact, a great question for young adults in the dating phase of their lives to ask a prospective mate is: "*Think of one of the most difficult experiences of your life. How did you manage it? Did you draw closer to the Lord? Or did you pull away from Him during that period of time?*" The answers can reveal some very useful information for one prospective mate about the other.

Nephi became more and more his true self by doing exactly what the Lord asked him to do—tough things that he might have avoided if he were to choose:

- *Retrieve the brass plates from Laban*—a trip to Jerusalem was about a 300-mile trip—one way. Nephi made the trip several times.
- *Behead Laban with Laban's own sword*—a hideous necessity that went against everything Nephi had been taught.
- *Build an oceangoing ship, but* not *after the manner of men*—something Nephi had no experience in doing.
- *Build a temple*—a task that had rarely been done in all the history of the world.

And through it all, Nephi held to his motto: "*I will go and do the things which the Lord hath commanded*" (1 Nephi 3:7).

I love the writings of Paul. Typically, Paul describes himself as *"an apostle of Jesus Christ"* (see Titus 1:1, for example). But in his epistle to Philemon, Paul describes himself in a most unusual way. He calls himself *"a prisoner of Jesus Christ"* (Philemon 1:1). Several years ago, I was studying that passage and I was a bit confused. Didn't the Savior come to free the captive? What did Paul mean he was "a prisoner of Jesus Christ"? Certainly Paul had been persecuted for his testimony of Christ—including imprisonment—but might there be another message? The more I thought about it, the more I understood Paul's wisdom; now I pray that I can be like him: a prisoner of the Lord Jesus Christ—meaning that *whatever* the Lord requires me to do, I will do. I will indeed go and do the things the Lord commands!

Would the real *you* please stand up?

How can you find out who you really are?
There is only one way:

By standing on the Lord's side of the line.

By standing up for His truths.

By doing all that the Lord requires of you.

Period.

What a different approach to personal growth and development this is than that prescribed by the world. Philosophers and psychotherapists might tell you to put on a backpack and journey to India; take a pilgrimage on a bike through France; hike to the top of Mount Everest; try hang gliding; take a class in a subject you've never studied before; go beyond the artificial bounds you have set for your abilities and talents; discover new things; uncover your passions. Although these may be useful in some ways, they miss the mark of really putting you in tune with your inner self, your spirit, your true self.

The world speaks about finding yourself through adventures that stretch you and your abilities. Well, obedience can be *quite* an adventure! Doing what the Lord wants you to do can take you places and into associations with people you never imagined!

A simple example: When you are given a visiting teaching or home teaching assignment to visit, take care of, and teach someone you've never met—and perhaps someone you may have never naturally gathered with—that can be a wonderful adventure—an adventure that can help you become more and more of your true self as you serve those you never would have otherwise known.

And just how obedient do you want to be? Read what Paul said of faithful Philemon:

"Having confidence in thy obedience I wrote unto thee, knowing that thou wilt also do more than I say" (Philemon 1:21).

Think about

Can you imagine the thrill you would feel if the Lord wrote those words about you? Imagine if you had such a history of obedience that the Lord could absolutely count on you—not merely to be obedient—but to do even more than He might require.

Be *more* obedient than you need to be and you will grow into who you really are even *more* quickly!

George Q. Cannon, who served as a counselor to four presidents of the Church, tells the following story:

"Many years ago I was in a very tight place financially, and I determined to put aside all I could as tithing. One day the Bishop of the Ward met me on the street and said: 'Brother George, you are paying a pretty good tithing.' 'No, Bishop,' said I, 'I am not paying the tithing of that which I have received; I am paying the tithing of that which I would like to receive.' And sure enough the next year I had as much income as I had paid tithing on the previous year."[5]

Bishop: "How is your personal scripture studying going?"

Brother: "Oh, Bishop I love the scriptures and read them every day."

Bishop: "Are you paying your tithing?"

Brother: "Absolutely. I need all the blessings I can get."

Bishop: "And what about the law of fasting. Do you fast? You understand that it means missing two meals."

Brother: "Oh, yes, Bishop, I keep the law of the fast. I normally eat only one meal every other day, so it takes me several days to fast—to miss two meals."

A bishop in Africa wanted to know how a new convert was doing. Their conversation unfolded something like this:

Bishop: "How are you enjoying attending your meetings?"

Brother: "Oh, I like coming to church. I never miss."

Bishop: "How do you like Sunday School?"

Brother: "I learn something every time. I am so grateful."

A fourteen-year-old boy in Bangalore, India, is on his way to growing into his true self. One Sunday morning during Aaronic Priesthood meeting, his teacher told the boys how he had missed the opportunity to serve a mission as a young man because he was too old when he joined the Church. Then a returned missionary told about his own opportunity to serve and the difference his mission had made in his life. As the returned missionary spoke with great emotion, the fourteen-year-old boy quietly, yet quickly, pulled a pen out of his pocket and wrote on his hand.

What did he write?

"Buy a pigey bank and start saving for mission."[6]

Does that remind you of the Primary song: "*When my mother calls me, quickly I'll obey*"? Well, during that particular priesthood meeting that great young man heard his Father call him, and he quickly obeyed and wrote on his hand what he needed to do—right now—to answer that call.

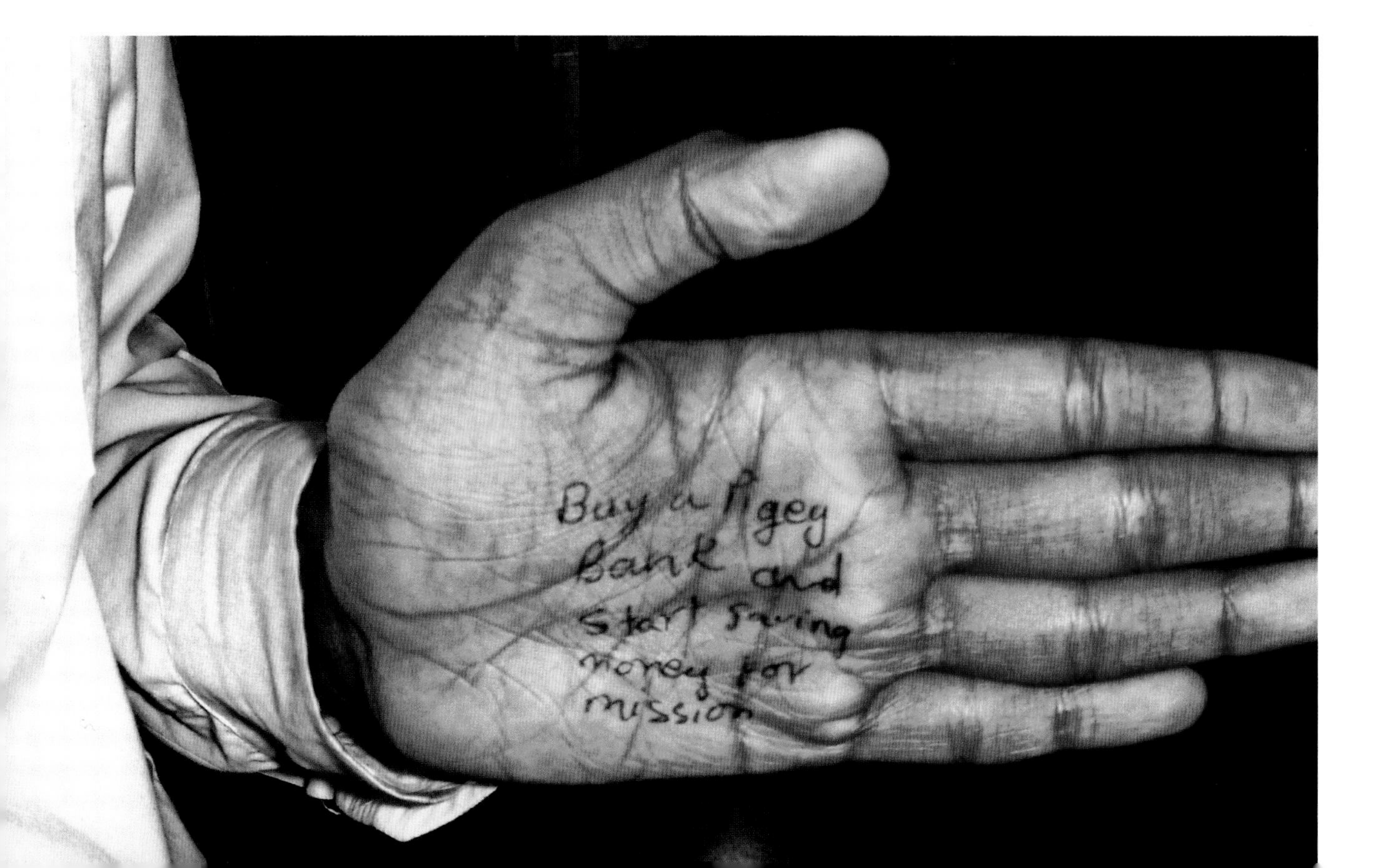

Principle #4: You can be your true self only when you are increasingly pure and leave the world behind.

As you come more and more out of the world,
you are free to be more of your true self.
As you are more of your true self,
you will desire to be less and less of the world.

It can be so easy to become hooked on the world.

I have a colorful jacket that is fun to wear. There are tiny inexpensive beads throughout the material that add just a hint of sparkle. And that's both the joy and the jeopardy of this jacket, which becomes a straitjacket for me every time I wear it! Why? Because the beads on the jacket often get snagged on a thread on the arm or body of the jacket, and I become immobilized. Depending upon where the "catch" takes hold, my arm is bound, and there is nothing I can do but hope that my husband has his Swiss army knife with him to cut the thread that is looped around one of the sparkly beads, and free me!

It doesn't take much to become hooked on the world.

It doesn't take much of the world in our lives to make us forget who we really are.

All the great desires of our hearts can be obliterated, all because of a little worldly snag.

Do you have a sparkly little "bead of sin" in your life that catches you off guard and holds you captive when you least expect it? It looks so innocent, so small. And it's so appealing.

Yes, you know it's worldly—but what's the big deal?

Well, the big deal is that it doesn't take much of the world's "sparkle and glitter" to immobilize us—to keep us from doing what we came to earth to do.

Just a shiny little worldly "bead" can prevent us from remembering who we are and from being our true selves!

Think about

Look around.
What small amount of
worldly glitter is keeping
you from being your
true self?

Principle #5: To be your true self, you need to stay immersed in truth and seek in every way to be infused with light!

A friend taught me a great truth long ago:

> The pictures we display in our homes bring a spirit. Make sure they bring the spirit that you want.

My husband and I had an unforgettable experience in Mongolia. We had the privilege of visiting a woman in her home—a circular tent structure, called a *ger,* no larger than fifteen feet in diameter. The interior was lovely and colorful; red and green wooden poles held up the canvas-and-felt structure and there was a red and green door. It was clean and tidy and well-organized. And also warm, on a cool (minus 33 degrees Celsius) February day.

Every space of this woman's home had a purpose: a kitchen area, a library with her scriptures readily available and some other great books to read, a place for her bed, an area to get ready for the day—including a mirror, and a place to dine.

And she had all the really important things when it came to pictures: a picture of the Savior, one of the prophet, and another of her family. And then she eagerly showed us something else: a framed certificate from the Hong Kong China Temple of her sealing for time and eternity to her deceased husband.

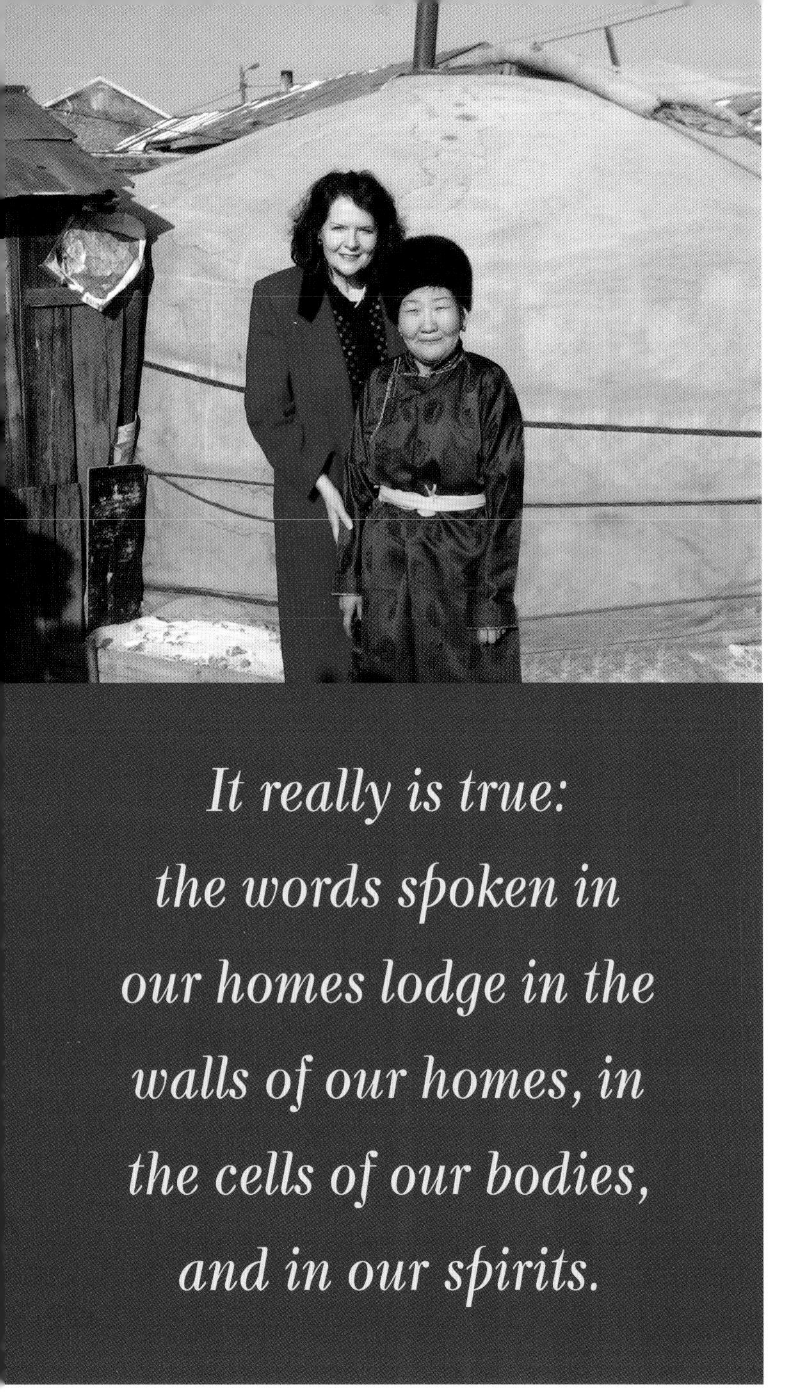

She had been born in that wonderful home, her *ger.* She had raised her children there. She had created a space where the Spirit of the Lord resided. All of the pictures in her home invited the Spirit and spoke the truth of where her heart and mind are.

The positive influence of this woman's home is evidenced in the lives of her children: Two daughters have served missions, and her son is preparing to leave on his.

One young wife and mother, desiring to do everything she could to bring peace and love and happiness into her home, began a practice of listening to the Book of Mormon while doing her housework. What a joy for her husband and children to walk in their home and experience those truths floating through the air.

When we are concerned about creating the best environment

- in which our children can learn,
- in which our marriages can prosper, and
- in which our spirits can be nurtured,

- and where all family members can emerge more and more as their true selves,

we should consider the powerful influence of the words of the Lord as they are spoken aloud in our homes.

> **When we are serious about immersing our lives in the Spirit and infusing our homes with the light and truth of the gospel, we will find a way to do it.**

One woman found that getting that "natural look" every morning before going out the door was taking longer and longer. She decided she would multitask and listen to the scriptures on audio and other inspirational CDs while getting ready for the day. What she may not have realized is that her countenance was becoming more lovely to look at—not because of the makeup she was applying, but because of the influence of the Spirit as she continued to immerse her mind and body in truth.

Immerse Your Sleep in Truths

A man, greatly desiring more light in his life and who had a history of having difficulty getting to sleep, even when he was exhausted, decided to listen to scriptures at a very soft level on his iPod. He was amazed at the deep, restorative sleep he enjoyed night after night as the words of the Lord permeated his mind as he drifted off to sleep.

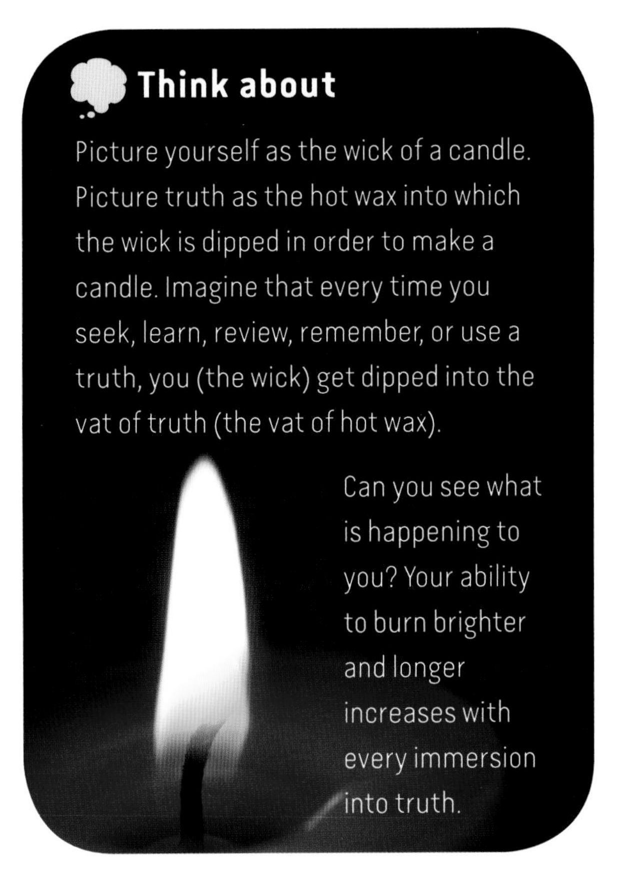

One woman, very serious about seeking more light and truth, decided to consecrate her life to the Lord and also to dedicate her sleep to Him. This is something that the Prophet Joseph Smith taught[7] and it's a pretty interesting idea.

Think about

- Would Moroni have been able to have nightly visits to Joseph Smith if the young Joseph had been listening to rock music on his iPod?
- Would Daniel have been able to hear what the angel Gabriel said to him if he were sleeping with a popular late-night TV show playing in the background? Would Daniel have heard, "O Daniel, I am now come forth to give thee skill and understanding" (Daniel 9:22)?
- Would Samuel have heard the Lord during the evening if he had been visiting worldly Web sites?
- Would we sleep and dream differently if we were to dedicate our sleep to the Lord?
- Would anything change if we slept without the TV on in the background?
- What difference would it make if we opened our scriptures and invited the Spirit into our bedrooms? Into our sleep?
- Is it possible to hear the voice of the Lord—even, or perhaps especially—as we sleep?

Consider the revelations and instruction that have come forth in dreams. Parenthetically, that can be another good reason for young (and perhaps, not so young) mothers to have a nap during the day or go back to bed in the morning after their children and husbands are off to school and work. They are not being lazy—they are gathering more information. They are dedicating their lives—even their sleep—to the Lord. They are seeking revelation to help strengthen them and their families—even in their dreams.

Think about

Elusive answers often emerge in the still of the night.

How many times have you solved a problem by sleeping? Have you ever awakened in the middle of the night with a clear answer to a question that had been troubling you all day?

Have you ever awakened at the beginning of a new day refreshed and ready to tackle an old problem anew?

Consider the number of times in the scriptures that people received instructions or warnings in dreams:

- Mary and Joseph were warned in a dream to flee to Egypt where they would be safe from Herod's army, who were coming to kill the young children of Israel (Matthew 2:13).
- Daniel received the interpretation of Nebuchadnezzar's dream in "a night vision" (Daniel 2:19).
- The Lord called the young boy, Samuel, to his ministry as Samuel "was laid down to sleep" (1 Samuel 3:3).
- Joseph Smith was visited during the night by Moroni, who revealed the existence of the gold plates to the young prophet (JS–H 1:30–47).

Try it

What might you discover if you dedicated your sleep to the Lord for twenty-one days? Try it! As part of your bedtime ritual, create an environment that is conducive to the Spirit. You will know what that involves for you as you pray about it. It may involve turning off the TV; watching or listening to something that is soothing to your spirit before bedtime; opening your scriptures and savoring one last morsel of truth before closing your eyes, and then leaving your scriptures open; counting your blessings—or alphabetizing them!—and expressing gratitude for everything, even for the wretchedly difficult things in your life.

Let the Lord know you are serious about dedicating your sleep to Him. Tell Him in your prayers. Let Him know you want to learn whatever He would have you learn—even in your sleep. And watch what happens.

What might you learn in the morning as you remain quiet for a moment before jumping out of bed? As you reflect to see if there is a dream or two you remember? Is there something you feel impressed to write down on a pad of paper by your bedside? What might you begin to learn about your true self?

What might happen as you pray for any and all instructions, directions, protections, and warnings that the Lord may be willing to give you as you sleep—perchance to dream?

THE STORY OF THE PHOENIX
RISING FROM THE ASHES
IS PURE MYTHOLOGY.

BUT YOU ARISING AS YOUR TRUE SELF
FROM THE ANGUISH AND
TERROR AND PAIN OF YOUR PRESENT
HEART-WRENCHING SITUATION
IS POSSIBLE AND TRUE!

Try it!

Let the five principles of this chapter help you to be more of your true self as you move forward—with faith—through whatever difficult circumstance you are in. You can do it!

Learn, repeat, and practice these five principles.

I can be my true self as I remove every obstacle that is preventing me from being my true self.

I can be my true self as I remember that I lived premortally.

I can be my true self as I am obedient to the Lord and am near to Him.

I can be my true self as I am increasingly pure and leave the world behind.

I can be my true self as I am immersed in truth and seek in every way to be infused with light.

Ask the Lord:

How can I be more of my true self at the end of this experience?

And listen for His answer.

QUESTION #7

WHAT DO I KNOW TO BE TRUE?

"Wendy, now that you're married, which of all those things ***on marriage*** *that you wrote when you were* ***single*** *would you change?"*

I've been asked this question several times since marrying.

It's a great question because our life experiences often change how we think about things.

A title of a book recently caught my eye: *What Have You Changed Your Mind About?*[1] The book was filled with the missteps and reconsiderations of high-powered thinkers who had previously proclaimed certain positions and ideas and who now, years later, had changed their minds and put forward some different ideas.

During my husband's medical training, his textbooks clearly warned: *"Do not touch the heart. It will stop beating!"* He had to go courageously and carefully against what was written in order to be a pioneer in the development of open heart surgery.

When new information becomes available or when research yields new results, we are obligated to consider what has been learned, and we may very well change our minds. Gratefully there are spiritual truths, which have been revealed to us, that remain constant and unchangeable.

So back to the earlier question: *"Which of all those things on marriage that you wrote when you were single would you change?"*

After hearing this question repeatedly, I did a quick search in my mental computer for what I had written and remembered the process I had gone through to write what I did.

My answer?

Actually, there is something I would change about those things I wrote, now that I'm married:

I WOULD PUT EVERYTHING IN NEON!

Think about

What are those things that you know to be true? That you would put in neon? What are those things that for you will *never* change and for which you are willing to take the witness stand?

What are the truths for which you would die? And, perhaps more importantly, what are the truths you will live by—under every condition? No matter what!

Write about

Write about *one* thing you know to be true.

How did you learn that truth?

When did you learn it?

What difference has that truth made in your life?

That truth, and others you know and will come to know, will anchor you when confusion and problems occur in your life.

That truth, and others you have learned, is something you can hold onto. Not just cling to, but hold fast to—just likethe iron rod. Something to repeat on really tough days. Something to reread and let register in your mind and heart one more time.

Which Truths Are Important?

Which truths can really make a difference in our lives? In the way we spend our time, talents, energy, and money? In the way we react to crises and long-term chronic difficulties? In the way we treat others, our bodies, the earth, and opportunities to serve, grow, and learn? In the way we seek more truths and live up to the privileges of the restored gospel of Jesus Christ? In short, which truths can really make a difference in the way we live our lives and in the joy we find in living?

Truths that support a growing faith in God are fundamental to a happy life. The Prophet Joseph Smith taught that each individual needs to know three truths to "exercise faith in God unto life and salvation":

"First, the idea that he actually exists.

"Secondly, a *correct* idea of his character, perfections, and attributes.

"Thirdly, an actual knowledge that the course of life which he is pursuing is according to his will."[2]

Think about

1. Do you know for yourself that God really lives?
2. Do you know for yourself His true nature?
3. Do you know for yourself that the course of life you are "pursuing is according to [God's] will?"[3]

If not, what are you doing to discover those three truths and remember them?

How Do You Respond to Truth?

People respond to truth in different ways

Think of Korihor, who, when offered the truth about God, responded in such a convoluted manner as to make listeners want to scratch their heads and say, *"Excuse me. Can you say that again?"*

Do you remember what Korihor said?

> *"I do not deny the existence of a God, but I do not believe that there is a God"* (Alma 30:48).

Note Korihor's guile. He cleverly dissuaded listeners from accepting the truth of God's existence by belittling and ridiculing such beliefs. *"Behold, these things which ye call prophecies, which ye say are handed down by holy prophets, behold, they are foolish traditions of your fathers. How do ye know of their surety? Behold, ye cannot know of things which ye do not see; therefore ye cannot know that there shall be a Christ"* (Alma 30:14–15).

Think of Amulek who, referring to his earlier lack of faith, said:

> *"I knew concerning these things, yet I would not know"* (Alma 10:16).

Sometimes truth scares us. Sometimes we are afraid to acknowledge what we know to be true—even to ourselves—because we don't want the responsibility that comes with knowing something is true. For example, the responsibility of updating our "catalog of truths" means discarding old ideas we have held on to for years and embracing new ones. We also might flee from truth because of the change in our behavior that is required—*"If such and such is true then I will need to behave in a different way."* That can be scary!

It takes courage to stand up for what we know to be true.

I think of a young woman in Edmonton, Alberta, Canada, who stood up during fast and testimony meeting. She had joined the Church a few years before and then had stopped attending. As she stood at the pulpit, she sounded like a counterpart to Amulek. (Remember he said, *"I knew . . . yet I would not know"* [Alma 10:6].)

This young woman said, *"I am here today to bear my testimony of the restored gospel of Jesus Christ because **now I know that I know**."*

Write about

What do you *know* that you know?

Write those truths down.

Keep adding to your list of "Things I Know to Be True."

Write about

- How you have responded to truth in the past
- How you now respond to truth
- How you want to respond to truth

How Can You Find Truth?

How can you know what is true? How can you keep adding to your treasure trove of truths?

Are you ready for a real adventure?

The Prophet Joseph Smith taught:

"The best way to obtain truth and wisdom is not to ask it from books, but to go to God in prayer, and obtain divine teaching."[4]

Truth-seeking requires work. Real work. Spiritual work. Persistent spiritual work. But what thrilling experiences await as you seek truth and wisdom in this way!

Just imagine what you will learn. You will learn truths that will influence your life forever—even for eternity—and you'll learn the process of learning those truths.

Both will be breathtaking.

Our lives change with every truth we embrace!

Our lives change as we increase our ability to receive more truth!

We can also learn truths through our experiences. Take time to reflect and note what you are learning through the joys and sorrows of your life. The Holy Ghost is the messenger of truth. You don't have to do this alone. He will guide you as you seek to learn what the Lord would have you learn from the experiences of your life. The Holy Ghost will help you have eyes to see, ears to hear, and a heart to understand.

***"The things of God** are of deep import; and time, and experience, and careful and ponderous and solemn thoughts can only find them out. Thy mind, O man! if thou wilt lead a soul unto salvation, must stretch as high as the utmost heavens, and search into and contemplate the darkest abyss, and the broad expanse of eternity—thou must commune with God!"*[5]

—Joseph Smith

Write about

Write the truths you are learning from the Lord and from your life.

From time to time take a moment, or an hour, and write down your thoughts about:

Truths I have learned lately and never want to forget

Try it

As you continue to add to your list of *Things I Know to Be True*—which will include *Truths I have learned lately and never want to forget*, let those truths, YOUR truths

- speak to your soul
- heal your heart
- unclutter your mind
- lift your spirit
- strengthen your resolve
- energize and invigorate you!

During times of stress or fear or hurt or discouragement or confusion or frustration, take a breath and ask yourself:

What do I know to be true?

Read your list.

Review your list.

Remember your list of *Things I Know to Be True*

and let each truth take root in your mind and penetrate your heart so that each can be healed.

What Can You Do If You Are in a Crisis and You Can't Find Your List?

Perhaps at that point all you can remember is that *you are a child of God*. Hold on to that truth.

How can that one simple, eternal truth help you with the stress, fear, and hurt of the present situation into which you have just been catapulted?

What good is just one truth? The answer is that *like attracts like,* as revealed in Doctrine and Covenants 88:40:

> *"For intelligence cleaveth unto intelligence; wisdom receiveth wisdom;* ***truth embraceth truth;*** *virtue loveth virtue; light cleaveth unto light; mercy hath compassion on mercy and claimeth her own."*

One truth attracts other truths. How marvelous is that? Let that work for you.

Following that pattern and principle, speak one truth to yourself: ***I am a child of God.*** And let that one truth attract another truth.

And let that next truth attract another.

What can happen if you don't follow that pattern?

- If you speak lies to yourself, those lies will attract other lies. So be very careful how you talk to yourself—throughout a typical day and in times of intense distress.
- If you speak fear, more fear will follow.

Like attracts like

- The angry expression of anger will engender more anger!
- Focusing on problems invites more problems to focus on.
- Focusing on solutions invites more solutions.
- Optimism attracts more optimism.
- Pessimism attracts more pessimism.
- Joy attracts joy.

Therefore, in times of stress or fear or hurt or discouragement or confusion or frustration, speak words of peace and safety and joy *and truth* to your soul.

The Conference Center was dedicated during the October 2000 general conference. At the close of that conference, President Gordon B. Hinckley pointed us in an important direction regarding the truths, the thoughts, and the words we invite into our minds. He said:

"The great 'Hosannah' salutation in which we participated this morning should remain an unforgettable experience. From time to time, we can repeat quietly in our minds, when we are alone, those beautiful words of worship."[6]

Beautiful words of worship are filled with power.

WORDS FILLED WITH POWER CAN BRING POWER TO OUR LIVES.

Think about

Imagine the power you can access as you recall the wording of the ordinances and covenants you have made with the Lord.

Let those words go through your mind from time to time. Your one-word replies have been recorded in heaven. The Lord won't forget—don't you. Review those promises in your mind and you will be strengthened against temptation and renewed in your determination to remain faithful.

Peace-filled words can bring you peace.

Holy words can bring holiness.

Powerful words can bring power.

Let's consider for a moment the concept of "power."

The Prophet Joseph Smith observed, "We have learned by sad experience that it is the nature and disposition of almost all men, as soon as they get a little authority [power], as they suppose, they will immediately begin to exercise unrighteous dominion" (D&C 121:39). We are taught that "No power or influence can or ought to be maintained . . . , only by persuasion, by long-suffering, by gentleness and meekness, and by love unfeigned" (D&C 121:41).

In addition, if "we undertake to cover our sins, or to gratify our pride, our vain ambition . . . [or if] any degree of unrighteousness [is present] . . . the heavens withdraw themselves; the Spirit of the Lord is grieved." And the ability to use the powers of heaven is lost (D&C 121:36–37).

You can't be truly powerful if you are coercive or oppressive.

You can't be truly powerful if you are not pure!

These truths might not be very popular in Hollywood, on Wall Street, or even on Main Street, but nevertheless they are true!

PURITY IS POWER

OBEDIENCE TO THE LORD IS POWER

RECEIVING HIS ORDINANCES IS POWER

MAKING AND KEEPING SACRED COVENANTS
WITH THE LORD IS POWER

FORGIVENESS IS POWER

APOLOGIZING IS POWER

REPENTING IS POWER

HUMILITY IS POWER

FAITH IS POWER

RIGHTEOUSNESS IS POWER

Write about

What have you come to know for yourself about power?

Definitions for power abound, but lately I am most drawn to the following:

"Power is the ability to do what the Lord needs you to do."[7]

If we are going to do what the Lord needs us to do,

We need power!

We need truth!

We need to remember what we know to be true!

Perhaps we need to ***take literally*** the scripture that teaches the powerful effect of having important things "always before our eyes" (Mosiah 1:5).

Try it

Post your list of "Things I Know to Be True" in a private place, but in a place that you can have them before your eyes daily. These are your very own "Articles of Faith," so to speak. As you sufficiently "retain in remembrance" (Alma 36:29) those things YOU know to be true, and as you let the power of those truths work on your mind and heart, you will have the strength to face the difficulties and tragedies of life, and you will have the power to do what the Lord needs you to do.

WE NEED TO IMMERSE OUR LIVES IN TRUTH

WE NEED TO SEEK TRUTHS

WE NEED TO SPEAK TRUTHS—TO OURSELVES AND TO OTHERS

WE NEED TO REMEMBER WHAT WE KNOW TO BE TRUE

WE NEED TO SHARE WHAT WE KNOW TO BE TRUE WITH THOSE WE LOVE

LET THE TRUTHS YOU KNOW AND LOVE CONNECT YOU WITH THE PEOPLE YOU KNOW AND LOVE!

One caution: We need to be careful how we share what we know to be true with others. We need to share with the utmost honoring of the law of agency.

I experienced the opposite of this on a recent trip to a former Communist country. On a gray, rainy day at the end of a lackluster tour of weary old buildings and other icons, punctuated with food that was barely palatable, the determined tour guide spoke loudly into the microphone on the tour bus:

"We have had a wonderful day together. We have seen the wonderful sights of the city and the wonderful treasures. And we have had wonderful weather and we shared a wonderful lunch together. This is my opinion and I believe that you are of the same opinion, too!"

As you honor the law of agency, you will experience joy as you share truth with others.

WHAT ARE THOSE THINGS THAT YOU KNOW TO BE TRUE?

WHAT ARE THOSE THINGS THAT YOU WOULD PUT IN NEON?

WHAT ARE THOSE THINGS THAT FOR YOU WILL *NEVER* CHANGE
AND FOR WHICH YOU ARE WILLING TO TAKE THE WITNESS STAND?

What are the truths for which you would die?

And, perhaps more importantly,

what are the truths you will live by

—under every condition?

NO MATTER WHAT!

CHAPTER 6 QUESTIONS, HEARTS, TRUTHS, AND THE LORD

One day my sister was talking on the phone to our niece in Canada. In the background was our niece's four-year-old daughter, Beth, busily playing as her mother chatted. Suddenly, in the middle of a very lengthy and enjoyable telephone conversation, our niece had to run to the next room to check on her baby boy. With her mother out of the room, little Beth seized the moment—and the telephone—and asked:

"Okay now, can we talk?

How are you doing—
really?"

Two great questions, out of the mouth of a child!
So unexpected and so purely genuine.
Such great questions that they immediately made my sister want to laugh and cry!

Great questions can do that!

Great Questions Can Build Great Relationships!

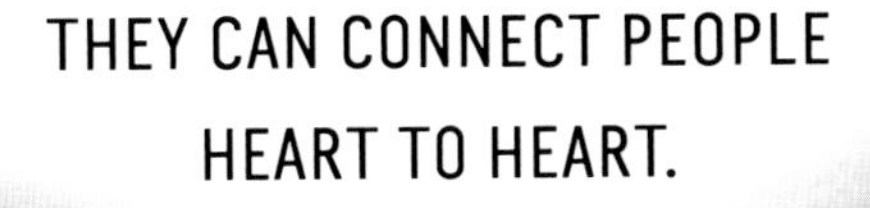

Just imagine how our lives would change if we would change our questions and only asked questions that showed others how much we care about them and how much we want to get to know their hearts!

Just imagine how our lives would change if we would just change our questions—and if we really listened to the questions that others ask!

Questions Can Reveal Another's Heart

It can be useful to listen carefully to the questions other people ask. Some questions can reveal a person's heart.

Consider these questions from the scriptures:

"How shall this be, seeing I know not a man?" (Luke 1:34)

Mary asked this question of the angel Gabriel, who had come to tell her that she was to be the mortal mother of the Savior of the world. Mary's question reveals her purity and then we see her unwavering faith in the Lord as she presents herself as His handmaid (Luke 1:38).

"Is it I?" (Matthew 26:22)

The apostles asked this question when the Savior said that one of them would betray Him. Their question reveals hearts focused on their own behavior rather than on accusing another.

"Whither shall I go that I may find ore?" (1 Nephi 17:9)

Nephi asked the Lord this question, revealing his willing heart to do whatever the Lord required of him—in this case, building a unique ship.

"Whither shall I go to obtain food?" (1 Nephi 16:23)

Nephi asked his father this question, revealing a heart that honored Lehi as a prophet of the Lord. This question also served as a useful wake-up call for Lehi after he had had a momentary crisis of faith.

"How shall we look when we are damned?" (Alma 14:21)

This question was used to taunt and mock Alma and Amulek, revealing the hard hearts of the people.

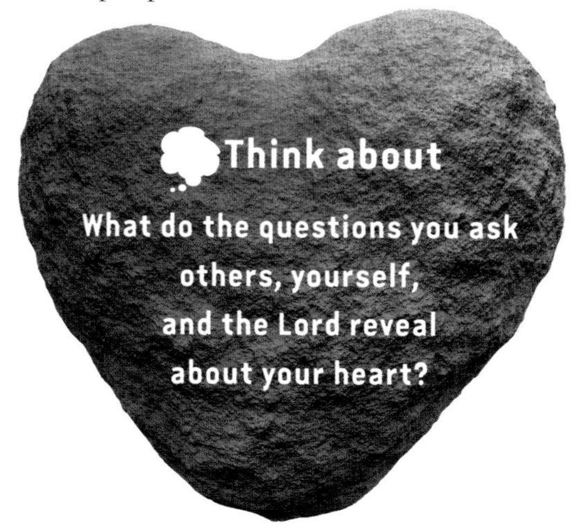

What else can great questions do?

Great Questions Can Introduce New Information

How can you invite someone to think about something new, something different?

Ask great questions!

People have been asking them for years.

Consider these questions from the Old Testament and the information embedded within them:

"Why sittest thou thyself alone, and all the people stand by thee from morning unto even?" (Exodus 18:14)

Moses' father-in-law asked Moses this question to introduce the need to delegate responsibility.

"Who knoweth whether thou art come to the kingdom for such a time as this?" (Esther 4:14)

Esther was asked this question, which rallied her focus and her courage to save her people.

"Where wast thou when I laid the foundations of the earth?" (Job 38:4)

God asked Job this question, establishing the greatness of God and the weakness of man.

"Did not we cast three men bound into the midst of the fire?" (Daniel 3:24)

King Nebuchadnezzar asked this question in amazement after his servants threw Shadrach, Meschach, and Abed-nego into the fire, testifying of the truth that he was witnessing a miracle.

"What could have been done more to my vineyard?" (Isaiah 5:4)

This question shows the great lengths to which the Lord has gone and will go in order to gather Israel home, as well as the grief He feels when he loses any of His children.

"O man, what is good; and what doth the Lord require of thee, but to do justly, and to love mercy, and to walk humbly with thy God?" (Micah 6:8)

This question teaches with clarity what the Lord requires of His children.

The Savior and Questions

Questions were asked *about* the Savior

People asked questions about the Savior from the beginning to the end of His mortal life. Consider just a few examples:

"Where is he that is born King of the Jews?" (Matthew 2:2)

The Wise Men asked this question as they searched for the baby Jesus.

"Can there any good thing come out of Nazareth?" (John 1:46)

Nathanael asked this question as the Savior's mortal ministry was beginning to unfold and be known. The question has now become a proverbial expression "of any unpopular or unpromising source of good."[1]

"Did not our heart burn within us?" (Luke 24:32)

"Why eateth your Master with publicans and sinners?" (Matthew 9:11)

The Pharisees disdainfully asked Jesus' disciples this question as part of their ongoing criticism of the Lord and His ministry.

"Shall I crucify your King?" (John 19:15)

Pilate sarcastically asked the Jews this question as part of the mocking preparation for the Savior's crucifixion.

"Why seek ye the living among the dead?" (Luke 24:5)

The angels asked Mary and the other women who came to the Lord's sepulchre this question.

"Did not our heart burn within us?" (Luke 24:32)

The disciples asked each other this question when they realized they had been in the presence of the resurrected Savior.

Write about

What questions do you ask about the Savior?

Questions were asked of the Savior

Questions that people asked provided the Savior a wonderful opportunity to teach and clarify some truths of His gospel.

"What sign shewest thou unto us, seeing that thou doest these things?" (John 2:18)

The priestly officials and rulers asked the Savior this question, seeking his credentials.

"How is it that thou, being a Jew, askest drink of me, which am a woman of Samaria?" (John 4:9)

"How can a man be born when he is old? can he enter the second time into his mother's womb, and be born?" (John 3:4)

The learned rabbi Nicodemus asked these two questions when he didn't understand what Jesus was trying to teach him.

"How is it that thou, being a Jew, askest drink of me, which am a woman of Samaria?" (John 4:9)

The woman at the well asked this question, wondering why He would speak to her.

"Let us alone; what have we to do with thee, thou Jesus of Nazareth? art thou come to destroy us?" (Mark 1:24)

The evil spirit that had possession of a man asked these questions.

"Who is my neighbour?" (Luke 10:29)

A young lawyer asked this question to justify his actions.

"Lord, Lord, have we not prophesied in thy name? and in thy name have cast out devils? and in thy name done many wonderful works?" (Matthew 7:22)

The Savior anticipates hearing these questions from many false priests and preachers, and less than faithful followers.

The Savior asked questions to prepare the people for His teachings

The following are a few of those questions.

"Art thou a master of Israel, and knowest not these things?" (John 3:10)

"Why reason ye these things in your hearts? Whether is it easier to say to the sick of the palsy, Thy sins be forgiven thee; or to say, Arise, and take up thy bed, and walk?" (Mark 2:8–9)

"Can the children of the bridechamber fast, while the bridegroom is with them?" (Mark 2:19)

"For had ye believed Moses, ye would have believed me: for he wrote of me. But if ye believe not his writings, how shall ye believe my words?" (John 5:46–47)

"Is it lawful to do good on the sabbath days?" (Mark 3:4)

Think about

What questions help you to prepare to learn more of the Savior's teachings?

Think about

The Savior taught with parables and with questions.

What truths did the Savior teach with the following questions?

- "How is it that ye sought me? wist ye not that I must be about my Father's business?" (Luke 2:49)
- "If ye then, being evil, know how to give good gifts unto your children, how much more shall your Father which is in heaven give good things to them that ask him?" (Matthew 7:11)
- "Whether is greater, he that sitteth at meat, or he that serveth?" (Luke 22:27)
- "What man shall there be among you, that shall have one sheep, and if it fall into a pit on the sabbath day, will he not lay hold on it, and lift it out? How much then is a man better than a sheep?" (Matthew 12:11–12)
- "Which now of these three, thinkest thou, was neighbour unto him that fell among the thieves?" (Luke 10:36)
- "Ought ye not to have done even as I commanded you, . . . and watched for my vineyard, and not have fallen asleep, lest the enemy should come upon you?" (D&C 101:53)

If the Savior asked the following questions of you, how would you answer?

Insert your name before each question, then read the question carefully. Pray to hear the voice of the Lord in your heart and mind as you read.

"________, what seek ye?" —JOHN 1:38

"________, wilt thou be made whole?" —JOHN 5:6

"________, why are ye fearful?" —MATTHEW 8:26

"________, why weepest thou?" —JOHN 20:13

"________, what wilt thou that I should do unto thee?" —MARK 10:51

"________, have I been so long time with you, and yet hast thou not known me?" —JOHN 14:9

"________, will ye also go away?" —JOHN 6:67

"________, lovest thou me?" —JOHN 21:16

"________, could ye not watch with me one hour?" —MATTHEW 26:40

God Wants Us to Ask Him Questions

When we are confused about what to do

We can heed the counsel of James:

"If any of you lack wisdom, let him ask of God" (James 1:5).

The Prophet Joseph Smith, as a fourteen-year-old boy, followed that counsel and went to a grove to ask the Lord which church to join. The answer he received was to join none of them. The answer—and all that followed to open the heavens for the last dispensation of the gospel of Jesus Christ—was bigger than the question!

When something is unclear to us

We can hear Nephi's question to his brothers ringing in our ears:

"Have ye inquired of the Lord?" (1 Nephi 15:8)

When we are desperate for an answer

We can hear the Lord's words:

"Ask, and it shall be given you" (Matthew 7:7).

In so many ways, the Lord asks us to ask Him.

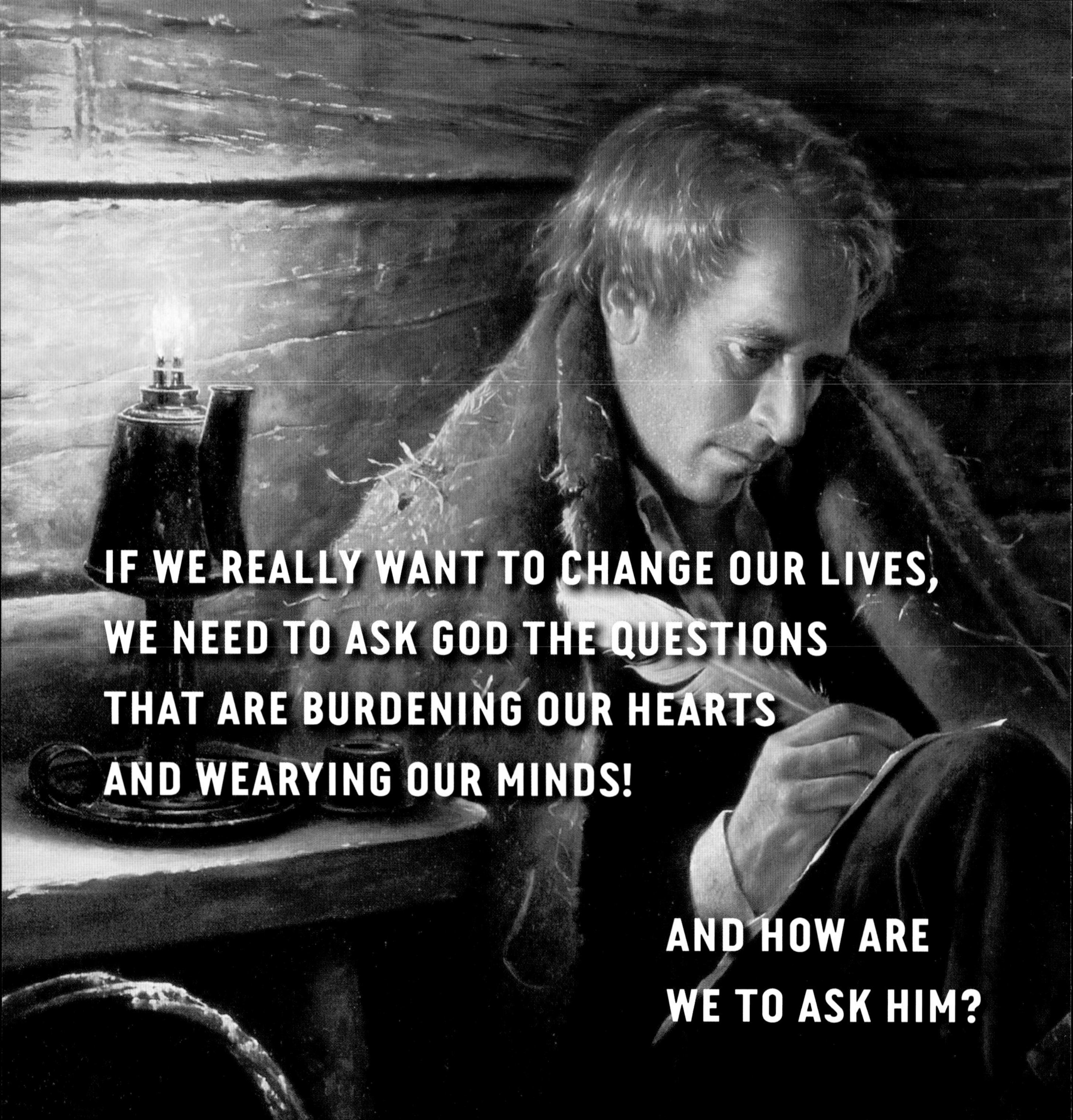
IF WE REALLY WANT TO CHANGE OUR LIVES,
WE NEED TO ASK GOD THE QUESTIONS
THAT ARE BURDENING OUR HEARTS
AND WEARYING OUR MINDS!
AND HOW ARE
WE TO ASK HIM?

WE ARE TO ASK GOD

- in faith (1 Nephi 15:11)
- in sincerity of heart (Mosiah 4:10)
- after studying things out in our minds (D&C 9:8)
- not asking amiss (2 Nephi 4:35)
- that which is right (Mosiah 4:21)
- believing that we will receive (Mosiah 4:21)
- in the name of Jesus Christ (3 Nephi 20:31)

AND GOD WILL ANSWER!

THROUGHOUT THIS BOOK WE HAVE FOCUSED ON CHANGING OUR LIVES BY CHANGING OUR QUESTIONS.

HOWEVER, IF WE REALLY WANT TO CHANGE OUR LIVES . . .

THERE IS ONLY ONE QUESTION WE NEED TO SEEK TO ANSWER HONESTLY WITH OUR WHOLE HEARTS, MINDS, AND LIVES!

I BELIEVE THE MOST IMPORTANT QUESTION WE COME TO EARTH TO ANSWER IS THIS ONE ASKED BY THE LORD HIMSELF:

"Whom say ye that I am?"

—Matthew 16:15

When we know the correct answer to that question everything in our life changes

Think about

Are there things in your life you want to change, things you need to do differently, to show that you know the answer is . . .

"Thou art the Christ,
the Son of the
living God."

—Matthew 16:16

The Savior did all that He did so that you and I can change and progress and become more and more like Him.

There is power in the Atonement to help us change our questions

and

change our lives!

NOTES

Chapter 1: The Power of Questions

1. Humberto R. Maturana and Francisco J. Varela, *The Tree of Knowledge: The Biological Roots of Human Understanding,* revised edition, translated by Robert Paolucci (Boston: Shambhala, 1992), 23.
2. Truman G. Madsen, *Joseph Smith the Prophet* (Salt Lake City: Bookcraft, 1989), 87.
3. Henry B. Eyring, "O Remember, Remember," *Ensign,* November 2007, 67, 69.
4. Henry B. Eyring, "'Always,'" *Ensign,* October 1999, 9.

Chapter 2: Questions, Problems, and Solutions

1. See Paul Wátzalwick, John H. Weakland, and Richard Fisch, *Change: Principles of Problem Formation and Problem Resolution* (New York: Norton, 1974).
2. See Karl Tomm, "Towards a Cybernetic-Systems Approach to Family Therapy," in D.S. Freeman, ed., *Perspectives on Family Therapy* (Vancouver, British Columbia: Butterworths, 1980).
3. See Luigi Boscolo and Gianfranco Cecchin, *Milan Group Family Therapy Workshop* (Audio, Video), Health Sciences Center, University of Calgary, Calgary, Alberta, Canada, March 1980.
4. Truman G. Madsen, *The Life and Teachings of the Prophet Joseph Smith* (Salt Lake City: Deseret Book, 2004, compact disc).
5. See Steve de Shazer, *Putting Difference to Work* (New York: Norton, 1991).
6. See Steve de Shazer and Insoo Kim Berg, "Constructing solutions," *The Family Therapy Networker* 12, no. 5 (1988): 42–43.
7. See Michael White and David Epston, *Narrative Means to Therapeutic Ends* (New York: Norton, 1990).
8. Ibid.

Chapter 3: Three Kinds of Questions

1. Dr. Karl Tomm, a pioneering professor in The Family Therapy Program within the Medical School at the University of Calgary, Calgary, Alberta, Canada, developed these three kinds of questions. See Karl Tomm, "Interventive Interviewing: Part II. Reflexive Questioning As a Means to Enable Self-Healing," *Family Process* 26 (1987): 167–83.
2. See Gregory Bateson, *Steps to an Ecology of Mind* (San Francisco, Calif.: Chandler Pub. Co., 1972).
3. See Tomm, *Family Process* 26 (1987): 167–83

Chapter 4: Beliefs and Questions

1. Two colleagues—Dr. Lorraine M. Wright and Dr. Janice M. Bell—and I developed this approach to problems at the Faculty of Nursing, the University of Calgary in Calgary, Alberta, Canada. We identified families we had worked with where greater change had occurred than anyone anticipated and where the improvements, after a significant period of time, had not only been sustained but increased. After an intensive analysis of our therapy sessions with the families, we came to the conclusion that core beliefs held by families are key to their problems and solutions. Our research led to the publication of the book *Beliefs: The Heart of Healing in Families and Illness* (New York: Basic Books, 1996). Drs. Wright and Bell published a book of their post-1996 experiences using our approach at the University of Calgary entitled *Beliefs and Illness* (Canada: Fourth Floor Press, 2009).
2. Lorraine M. Wright, Wendy L. Watson, and Janice M. Bell, *Beliefs: The Heart of Healing in Families and Illness* (New York: Basic Books, 1996), 19.

3. I developed this hypothetical question which "embeds a facilitative belief and is an indirect way of challenging or altering a constraining belief. The hypothetical nature of the question invites a sense of playfulness and experimentation with a new way of thinking. . . . [T]here is something about the hypothetical subjunctive mood of the 'if you were to believe' question . . . that invites people in a gentle yet powerful manner to consider an alternative facilitative belief, a belief often diametrically opposed to their current constraining belief" (Wright, Watson, and Bell, *Beliefs*, 194).

Chapter 5: Seven Questions That Can Change Your Life

Question 1: What Is on My Premortal List of Things to Do While on Earth?

1. Joseph Smith, *History of The Church of Jesus Christ of Latter-day Saints*, 7 vols., introduction and notes by B. H. Roberts (Salt Lake City: The Church of Jesus Christ of Latter-day Saints, 1932–1951), 6:50). Joseph Smith taught: "Could we read and comprehend all that has been written from the days of Adam, on the relation of man to God and angels in a future state, we should know very little about it. Reading the experience of others, or the revelation given to them, can never give us a comprehensive view of our condition and true relation to God. Knowledge of these things can only be obtained by experience through the ordinances of God set forth for that purpose. Could you gaze into heaven five minutes, you would know more than you would by reading all that has ever been written on the subject."
2. Have you noticed that much of our testing involves learning to control our bodies' appetites and passions, some of which can get out of control or become distorted through various forms of abuse?
3. Joseph F. Smith, *Gospel Doctrine: Selections from the Sermons and Writings of Joseph F. Smith*, compiled by John A. Widtsoe (Salt Lake City: Deseret Book, 1939), 249; emphasis added.
4. See Truman G. Madsen, *Timeless Questions, Gospel Insights* (Salt Lake City: Bookcraft, 1998, audio cassette).
5. Orson F. Whitney, *Saturday Night Thoughts* (Salt Lake City: Deseret News, 1921), 294–95.
6. Personal communication with Elder Russell M. Nelson.

Question 2: What Is the One Question I Most Need to Have Answered from the Scriptures Today?

1. See Brigham Young, in *Journal of Discourses*, 26 vols. (London: Latter-day Saints' Book Depot, 1854–1886), 10:251.
2. In working with families with health problems, Dr. Lorraine M. Wright created the "one question question" to uncover a family's most pressing concern. See Lorraine M. Wright, "When Clients Ask Questions: Enriching the Therapeutic Conversation," *The Family Therapy Networker* 13, no. 6 (1989): 15–16.
3. Personal communication with Elder Russell M. Nelson.

Question 3: What Are Three Words to Follow for a Great Life?

1. It is not possible to list all the possible pornographic influences.
2. E. R. Lolo, "Not Even Once." Used by permission.

Question 4: Whose Agenda Is This Supporting?

1. Jeffrey R. Holland, "To Young Women," *Ensign*, November 2005, 29; emphasis in original.
2. See Dallin H. Oaks, "Pornography," *Ensign*, May 2005, 87–90. Elder Oaks appealed to women saying, "Please

understand that if you dress immodestly, you are magnifying this problem by becoming pornography to some of the men who see you" (*Ensign,* May 2005, 90).

Question 5: If I Were to Pray for and Picture the Holy Ghost Being Right Beside Me, How Would I Manage This Difficult Situation?

1. Brigham Young, *Journal of Discourses,* 26 vols. (London: Latter-day Saints' Book Depot, 1854–1886), 2:255.

Question 6: How Can I Be More of My True Self at the End of This Experience?

1. Personal communication with Truman G. Madsen.
2. Sheri Dew, "Knowing Who You Are—And Who You've Always Been," in *Ye Shall Bear Record of Me: Talks from the 2001 BYU Women's Conference* (Salt Lake City: Deseret Book, 2002), 278.
3. P. Scott Richards and Allen E. Bergin, *A Spiritual Strategy for Counseling and Psychotherapy* (Washington, DC: American Psychological Association, 1997), xi.
4. James Ira Young, "Who Am I?" Used by permission.
5. George Q. Cannon, *Gospel Truth: Discourses and Writings of President George Q. Cannon,* selected, arranged, and edited by Jerreld L. Newquist (Salt Lake City: Deseret Book, 1987), 512.
6. Personal communication with Elder Kent D. Watson.
7. Truman G. Madsen, *The Life and Teachings of the Prophet Joseph Smith* (Salt Lake City: Deseret Book, 2004, compact disc).

Question 7: What Do I Know to Be True?

1. *What Have You Changed Your Mind About? Today's Leading Minds Rethink Everything,* edited by John Brockman (New York: HarperCollins, 2009).
2. Joseph Smith, *Lectures on Faith* (Salt Lake City: Deseret Book, 1985), 3:2.
3. Ibid.
4. Joseph Smith, *Teachings of the Prophet Joseph Smith,* selected and arranged by Joseph Fielding Smith (Salt Lake City: Deseret Book, 1976), 191.
5. Ibid., 137.
6. Gordon B. Hinckley, "'An Humble and a Contrite Heart,'" *Ensign,* November 2000, 89.
7. Anonymous.

Chapter 6: Questions, Hearts, Truths, and the Lord

1. James E. Talmage, *Jesus the Christ* (Salt Lake City: Deseret Book, 1983), 111.

ACKNOWLEDGMENTS AND CREDITS

Heartfelt gratitude to Jana Erickson and her editing and design team: Richard Erickson, Tonya Facemyer, Shauna Gibby, Kayla Hackett, Barry Hansen, Lisa Mangum, Richard Peterson, Sheryl Dickert Smith, Heather G. Ward

Artwork Credits

Page 1: "The First Vision" © Greg Olsen. By arrangement with Greg Olsen Art Publishing Inc., Meridian, Idaho, 83642. For information on art prints by Greg Olsen, please contact Greg Olsen Art Publishing Inc. at 1–208–888–2585.

Page 32: "Trail of Hope . . . Last Hill" by Al Rounds. Used by permission.

Page 108: Detail from "Ascension" by Mark Mabry. Used by permission.

Page 130: "An Obscure Boy" by Joseph Brickey. Used by permission.

Page 136: Detail from "I Am the Way" by Simon Dewey. Used by permission.

Page 145: "Let Him Ask of God" by Jon McNaughton. Used by permission.

Page 256: "Road to Emmaus" by Mark Mabry. Used by permission.

Page 257: "Living Water" by Simon Dewey. Used by permission.

Page 262: "Liberty Jail" © Greg Olsen. By arrangement with Greg Olsen Art Publishing Inc., Meridian, Idaho, 83642. For information on art prints by Greg Olsen, please contact Greg Olsen Art Publishing Inc. at 1–208–888–2585.

Page 266: Detail from "Teacher" by Mark Mabry. Used by permission.

Pages 268–69: "Resurrection" by Mark Mabry. Used by permission.

Photo and Image Credits

Image Source/Getty Images: 213

iStock: 19, 55, 62, 72, 86, 88, 91, 92, 96, 99, 103, 104, 106, 107, 112, 113, 114, 115, 116, 117, 118, 119, 125, 126, 127, 128, 129, 131, 133, 135, 138, 140, 141, 142, 143, 144, 149, 151, 152, 154, 178, 179, 185, 186, 188, 189, 194, 195, 196, 198, 201, 207, 209, 210, 211, 214, 217, 218, 220, 224, 227, 232, 233, 236, 237, 239, 241, 242, 247, 248, 249, 258

Jupiter Unlimited: 7, 23, 31, 33, 37, 40, 44, 47, 51, 52, 54, 56, 58, 59, 61, 63, 64, 65, 70, 71, 72, 73, 76, 85, 93, 94, 95, 97, 111, 114, 153, 161, 170, 171, 174, 175, 176, 180, 183, 184, 206, 228, 251, 259

Shutterstock: 2, 8, 14, 15, 16, 17, 18, 20, 21, 24, 25, 27, 28, 29, 34, 35, 36, 42, 45, 46, 48, 49, 50, 57, 60, 66, 76, 78, 81, 82, 83, 84, 90, 95, 98, 100, 101, 102, 109, 120, 135, 137, 139, 146, 156, 157, 160, 164, 166, 168, 169, 171, 173, 174, 182, 187, 193, 216, 221, 229, 231, 235, 240, 244, 246, 252, 253, 254, plus all "Think about," "Try it," and "Write about" icons

Additional photos and images provided by:
Karyn Card Butler, Bradley Watson Card, Rebecca Card Closson, Amanda Card Croft, Laurie Cook, Elder Donald L. Hallstrom, Wendy Watson Nelson, Cynthia Card Smith, Elder Kent D. Watson, Lorraine Mae Wright, Trisha Zemp